WORKSHOP WONDERS

The Ultimate Guide to Rotation Sunday School

BY MICKIE O'DONNELL AND VICKIE BARE

NEXGEN®

Building the New Generation of Believers

AN IMPRINT OF COOK COMMUNICATIONS MINISTRIES
Colorado Springs, Colorado • Paris, Ontario
KINGSWAY COMMUNICATIONS, LTD
Eastbourne, England

NexGen® is an imprint of
Cook Communications Ministries, Colorado Springs, CO 80918
Cook Communications, Paris, Ontario
Kingsway Communications, Eastbourne, England

WORKSHOP WONDERS
The Ultimate Guide to Rotation Sunday School
Copyright © 2005 Cook Communications Ministries

Writers: Mickie O'Donnell, Vickie Bare
Editor: Lois Keffer
Art Direction: Nancy L. Haskins
Cover Design: Nancy L. Haskins, Lois Keffer, Lisa Pence
Interior Design: Sandy Flewelling
Cover Photos: © Stockbyte, © Comstock, © Digital Vision

Printed in the United States of America
First printing, 2005
1 2 3 4 5 6 7 8 9 10   07 06 05

ISBN 0781442087

Dedications

· ·

To all those moms who wonder how to provide
a dynamic ministry for their own children,
and then become Christian Educators.
You can do this—we did!

— *Mickie and Vickie*

To my husband, Frank, who wonders
what in the world I actually do,
but who supports me multidimensionally!

— *Mickie O'Donnell Gutierrez*

To my wonderful husband, Greg,
and my kids, Travis and Chelsea.
Thanks for believing in me.
— *Vickie Bare*

About the Authors

Vickie Bare is the Director of Children's Ministry at Christ Church of Oak Brook in Oak Brook, Illinois. A daughter of the Republic of Texas, Vickie graduated from the University of Texas at Austin in 1980 with a Bachelor of Arts in English and French with a Professional Sequence in Education.

After teaching middle school for seven years in Round Rock, Texas, Vickie stayed at home with her two children, Travis and Chelsea. Encouraged by Mickie O'Donnell, she joined the staff at Christ Church in 1999 to help establish a rotation Sunday school program. With the Holy Spirit as her tutor, Vickie continues to write, implement and refine as she lovingly disciples the children in her ministry. The outgrowth of this work is *Workshop Zone*™ curriculum, a five-year rotational/multidimensional Sunday school program published by Cook Communications Ministries.

God has used Vickie's passion for planting seeds for the kingdom in kids' lives to build a dynamic children's ministry. She is a cherished mentor both to children and to colleagues in children's ministry. Vickie lives in Hinsdale, Illinois with her husband, Greg, her kids, Travis and Chelsea, and her Shih Tzu, Patches.

Mickie O'Donnell Gutierrez has worked in Christian Education in the local church since 1976. She is a graduate of The University of Aberdeen Scotland, with a Masters of Philosophy and Trinity Divinity School with a Masters of Religious Education. She has served as Minister of Christian Education at Westhill Christian Fellowship in Aberdeen Scotland, Village Presbyterian Church in Northbrook, Illinois and as Director of Children's Ministries at Christ Church of Oak Brook in Oak Brook, Illinois.

Mickie has been an adjunct faculty member of Trinity International University and is currently adjunct faculty with Illinois Benedictine University. In addition to writing extensively on multidimensional learning, she has contributed a chapter on Play Therapy in the book *Healing the Children of War* (1995, Marc Publishing).

As one of the original educators promoting multidimensional/rotational learning experiences, she has edited Children's Ministries of America's Handbook (a best practices manual) and served as a consultant to several publishers. Currently Mickie is President of Lord and King Associates, Inc. which presents the yearly International Conference on Multidimensional Learning, (CMA Conference), a rallying point of encouragement and inspiration for those who teach God's children. Lord and King Associates, Inc. produces training videos and seeks out resources to help churches across the country revitalize their Sunday schools. Mickie's faithfulness to her vision has brought renewed life and hope to churches across the nation.

Acknowledgments

Remembering to thank all of the people who have influenced the journey that equipped me to write this book seems impossible. My greatest cheerleaders and encouragers have been my family, my friends and the incredible staff at Christ Church.

For her honest spiritual direction and patient coaching, many thanks to Adele Calhoun. Thanks as well to John Klingelhofer, Doug Calhoun, and Mike Murphy for serving as sounding boards and helping me refine my understanding of God's Word. My senior pastor, Dan Meyer, and my executive pastor, Greg Ogden, set a vision before me that both inspired and challenged me. And Andy Morgan, who supported me from the start of this ministry, empowered me and protected me from many storms. Indeed, the entire staff at Christ Church is truly woven into the fabric of this book.

In all seasons of this journey, my Ya Yas, Charla Russell, Dawn Reinhart, Delene Kirtland and Nancy Rose, have supported me with prayer and encouragement. They have been Jesus to me more times than I can count. Lois Keffer has been a gentle teacher who has stretched me beyond my wildest imaginings. Mickie O'Donnell gave me a great gift when she saw my future in Children's Ministry long before I did. The workshop leaders and shepherds who have been on the front lines gave invaluable feedback as my partners in ministry. My greatest teachers have been the children in my ministry who have allowed me to see God through eyes unclouded by dogma and unfettered by regulations.

Finally, I save my dearest expression of gratitude and love for my husband, Greg, and my children, Travis and Chelsea. You bless and enrich my life beyond measure.

— *Vickie Bare*

My contribution to this book has grown from interaction with the incredible children who have waltzed through my 25-plus years in children's ministry and my colleagues in multidimensional learning who have honed these concepts with me. Without these experts there would be no grassroots movement: Bob and Joyce Claus, Jan Hubbard, Mary Jane Huber, Pam Myers, Jim and Beth Wagner and Jack and Peggy Gilmour. Thanks to Neil MacQueen and Melissa Hansche for sharing ideas they gleaned from material published by Cook Communications Ministries in the mid-90s that helped us develop the concept beyond anyone's imagination.

I want to acknowledge other educators and experts: Jill Bennett, Deborah Cummins, Viv Houk, Jean Blaydes-Madigan, Jan Snell, Cathy Soldner, David Titus, Deb Veit, Deb Wagner, John Walsh, Todd and Julie Weiland, Ken and Phyllis Wezeman, Dennis Wilson and the many others who give selflessly of their time and talents each year for the

National Conference. You will recognize some of your stories in this book!

Thanks to my best friend, Holly Schmid, who spearheaded the Children's Committee at The Village Presbyterian Church in Northbrook in the mid-90s and helped make "The Kingdom" a reality. Without her persistence and faith this concept would not have taken flight.

Very special thanks to my family. My son Joel's learning challenges encouraged me to look for new and better ways to reach children with the Gospel message. How I wish this model had been around when you and your siblings were growing up. My parents, Bob and C.A. O'Donnell, live out their faith in Christ multidimensionally and continue to embrace God's grace with an attitude of wonder. It is from their living testimony that I came to faith.

Heartfelt gratitude goes to my writing partners, Vickie Bare and Lois Keffer. These brilliant women have inspired and challenged me. Without them, my words would never have rested on the page. It has been an honor to work with them.

Finally, a big thank-you goes to my husband, Frank. While he continues to wonder what I actually do for a living, he has supported me and given me the freedom and time to devote myself to this passion.

To the people of Cook Communications Ministries, thank-you for "getting it!" May this book help adults both now and in the future transform the educational ministry of the church for the sake of God's kingdom.

— *Mickie O'Donnell Gutierrez*

Contents

"It's time we stopped instructing children, but instead built constructs from within which they can have authentic experiences of God."

—*Walter Wangerin,*
speaking at the Children's Spirituality
Conference, Concordia University, 2003

Introduction:

The Birth of a Movement

In the late 1980s a handful of Chicago area Directors of Christian Education met for mutual support and encouragement. In the course of their conversations, mutual frustrations came to light. Why did so few people seem to be growing in their faith? Why did children struggle in Sunday School? What happened to all the enthusiasm Vacation Bible School generated—why didn't it carry into the rest of the church year?

In God's good timing, Cook Communications Ministries published a new style of Bible school material called VeBs, "Very exciting Bible School." It was a site-based concept, just a bit different from the norm. This new material allowed teachers to stay in one location and teach the same lesson each day to different groups of children. Each site had a unique story, song, craft and snack.

Throughout the week, the children rotated from room to room to experience what each location offered.

A few of us in the Chicago area used this VeBS material and were intrigued by the fact that the children were engaged and happy while the leaders enjoyed preparing a single lesson rather than scrambling to prepare something new each day. Several educators looked at the success of VeBS and wondered if it might be a model for Sunday school year round.

At the same time, the Learning Styles theory was gaining wide spread acceptance in the educational community. Our group of Christian educators wondered aloud about using the concept of VeBS and blending it with Learning Styles. We began to develop a new model for our Sunday schools with rooms that were specific to learning styles, teachers who taught in a specific room and children rotating to various rooms each week. This method allowed for teaching a story in depth over a series of weeks rather than skimming the top and jumping to a new story each Sunday.

In the early 1990s another group of Chicago area Christian educators began experimenting with a similar idea. The Chicago Presbytery's magazine published an article titled "Sunday School Run Amuck," which featured Neil MacQueen and Melissa Hansche's Sunday school ministry, "The Doors." A visit to their Sunday school made it clear to all of us that God's Spirit was moving us to try something new in order to revive not just Sunday school, but the entire educational ministry of the church.

Delighted with the great enthusiasm we saw in our children and staff, and encouraged with the impact this new approach was having on the lives of our kids, several of us continued to meet to share ideas and inspiration. Good news travels, and soon inquiries began pouring in from across the county. Responding to these inquiries began to drain energy and time from our local ministries, so in May of 1995 we planned a one-day event to allow others a firsthand look at how these innovations were revolutionizing our Sunday schools. To our surprise, over 70 pastors and educators from all over the United States flew in to explore this exciting new movement!

That day produced a small but meaningful discovery. One church called their new ministry "The Doors." Doors painted in different colors designated rooms devoted to certain types of learning activities. At Mickie's church, the newly designed children's ministry area suggested an entry to heaven and was called "The Kingdom." Two educators from nearby Arlington Heights joined us that day. To everyone's astonishment, they had titled their program "The Kingdom Doors"! At that moment we realized that God was behind this growing phenomenon; we were privileged to be part of it.

That core group in Chicago made a commitment to meet, share, pray and teach others what God was teaching us. We quickly began to see that God was using these innovative concepts in teaching to bring new life not only to Sunday school, but also to whole churches! As members of the initial group moved into publishing, software development and church school design, they appointed Mickie to organize a National Conference on Multidimensional Learning to address the training and support needs of this growing movement.

That was the beginning. We continue to see hundreds of new churches attend conferences and training events each year. Our tiny mustard seed has grown to a flourishing tree of renewal and refreshment in Christian Education!

Sunday school has always been about finding the best possible ways to reach children with the life-changing message of God's Word. Through the years Christian publishing companies have worked hard to provide the best possible resources. Caring, creative teachers have tweaked those materials to suit the particular needs of their students. In this sense, multidimensional/rotational learning is not something entirely new. It is simply a fresh paradigm based on our growing understanding of how kids learn. Its purpose is to make disciples as Jesus instructed, by giving kids memorable experiences with the Word.

What drives us to find new, creative ways to present the Bible to kids? Simply this. Each year we learn more and more about how God has programmed us to learn. As we utilize the multiple pathways God has put at our disposal, the impact of our teaching takes on a whole new dynamic. Multidimensional learning can be utilized not only in a rotational format for Sunday school, but also within traditional contained classrooms and in large group/small group settings.

The question before each of us is: "Are we using all the intelligences to convey the message of God's story, to let it sink deep into children's minds and hearts?" Spending weeks on the same story gives children the maximum opportunity to experience the story in ways that will expand their knowledge of God and grow their tender, young faith. So while this model may provide the richest learning environment, there are many ways to be multidimensional in teaching God's Word.

In this book Vickie and I offer insights and practical advice we've gained through years of teaching in this dynamic environment. We pray that what we offer will challenge and encourage you to step away from comfortable, familiar patterns of Sunday school. See how God can transform the lives of children through the wonders of multidimensional workshops that teach God's Word in ways that God created children to learn.

**"See, I am doing a new thing! Now it
springs up; do you not perceive it?
I am making a way in the desert and
streams in the wasteland."**
Isaiah 43:19

In God's service with you,
Mickie O'Donnell Gutierrez

1 How God Made Kids

With tears in his eyes the father shared what his son experienced upon baking his creation.

The Monday after Easter one of my parent volunteers came into my office. He was eager to tell me about his third grader's experience after Sunday school the day before. In our Easter study, kids made Resurrection Buns. Each step in preparing the buns was symbolic of Jesus' ordeals: children pounded and rolled dough, chopped nuts, pressed nuts into the dough, sprinkled on vinegar, cinnamon and sugar, placed marshmallows on the dough, then rolled it up and pinched it shut. We told the children to take their buns home, bake them, and report what happened. With tears in his eyes the father shared what his son experienced upon baking his creation.

"We were at my parents'," he said, "and my son insisted that his grandmother take the roast out of the oven so he could bake his marshmallow *bun. We sat in the living room and talked while he patiently waited for his bun to bake. Suddenly he came running in with a half-eaten hollow bun exclaiming, 'Look—Jesus is gone! He's alive!' I knew that my son had experienced the resurrection in a much more profound way than if he had just heard the story. Thank you for this new way of teaching."*

Picture the children in your ministry. The freckle-faced turbo-charged boy whose enthusiasm is bested only by his inability to focus and keep from distracting his classmates. The quiet girl who creates masterpieces of art when given the opportunity, but finds it painfully difficult to speak up. The class clown who has an irrepressible knack for making everything dramatic and fun. The thoughtful child who seldom responds without prompting, but contributes astounding insights when called on. The child who sings like an angel (if indeed angels sing); the one who moves to a non-stop inner sense of rhythm. The one who eats Bible memory verses whole and spits them back to you with unfailing perfection. The one who is a friend to children whom others tend to ignore. The one who is so eager to please that he's always at your side. The one who has been hurt by life and sits quietly each week, shut inside herself.

They're diverse, loving, lovable and exasperating. They have an insatiable hunger to know and try new things. They long for their achievements to be acknowledged. They're unique and precious in God's sight. And you have them for an hour or less each week. How effectively are you using that hour?

Reality Check

The catalyst for change in my (Mickie's) approach to children's ministry was finding a major disconnect between my goals and the results I was seeing. Some of my most jolting reality checks came not from kids themselves, but from parents and teachers.

A phone call from the irate mother of two boys in my Sunday school brought one such dose of reality. "Why is it," she asked, "that every time I bring my boys to Sunday school all they come home with is Bible, Bible, Bible? Why aren't you teaching them good manners and other stuff that would be more useful?" I was stunned. I thought to myself, "How is it that this mother has entirely missed the objective of Christian education?"

Then there was the busy Lenten season when I found myself on the phone once again, making a round of calls to fill the gaps in my Sunday school staff. One dear soul, a pillar of the church, agreed to fill the need. But before I could even breathe a sigh of relief, she asked me, "Why do we call Good Friday 'good'?" I shook my head and took a deep breath. Here is a woman, I thought to myself, who has been in church all her life, has taught Sunday school for years, is the mother of three grown children, has sat on virtually every committee at this church. Yet she is clueless about this basic fundamental of the Christian faith. How could this happen? And what will the children in her class learn in that fleeting hour on Sunday morning?

As a Christian educator I knew my purpose: to bring people of all ages to a maturity of Christian faith that would be demonstrated in their attitudes and actions. But many of the people I encountered at church fell far short of those expectations. They lacked basic Bible knowledge. They did not understand how to approach life with a Christian worldview. Well-meaning teachers were passing their ignorance to the next generation.

If I was to succeed in my goal of teaching kids to be true disciples of Jesus, something needed to change. All my hard work and that of my staff was bringing disappointing results. Somehow we were failing to pass the faith story from one generation to the next. I didn't want to fail God's kids. I knew it was my responsibility to make the very best use of that hour they spent in Sunday school. Yet attendance was so sporadic that I despaired of giving them a sound understanding of God's Word.

I knew that real learning required review and reinforcement, but how could I build on a lesson kids had missed?

Recruiting teachers was an ongoing struggle. I settled for filling slots with volunteers who lacked the gifts to cover all the aspects of teaching a lesson. I used good Bible-based curriculum that gave a variety of teaching options, but my teachers skimmed the surface of the Bible truth as they flew through the lessons, trying to cram everything into an hour. Each week I had to deal with bored, disruptive children and discouraged volunteers. The pastoral staff seemed to feel that my main task was to keep the children busy while the rest of the "real church" went about worshiping, fellowshiping and drinking coffee and dunking doughnuts.

A Hopeful Beginning

Discomfort is a great catalyst for change! God used these challenges to pry me out of familiar patterns and drive me to find more effective ways of teaching His kids. It was clearly time to bring to bear our growing understanding of how kids learn, and put that knowledge to use in teaching kids what it means to follow Jesus.

And so, a few Chicago area pioneers banded together to create a new model for Sunday school—a model known alternatively as workshop rotation and multidimensional learning. Our first efforts brought wonderful results. Kids relished the smorgasbord of Bible learning activities that awaited them each week. Volunteers with specific gifts to offer found great delight in teaching to their strengths. Staffing issues disappeared as workshop leaders started coming out of the woodwork. A peek in any classroom revealed kids totally engaged in challenging learning experiences.

Was it quick and easy? No. We were making it up as we went, writing like crazy, learning with the kids, and sharing with each other our successes and failures. Sunday mornings were charged with positive energy. We were on to something, and God was blessing it!

Good news travels. Our networks grew and flourished. Suddenly we were riding the swell of a grassroots movement that was revitalizing Sunday schools across the nation. As of this writing, thousands of churches across the United States have adopted the workshop rotation/multidimensional learning model. They're reaping the benefits of revitalized Sunday schools, enthusiastic support from their congregations, and children whose faith is growing, deeply rooted in God's Word.

As churches move into multidimensional learning, we get reports like these.

> **"Not only has our Sunday school increased in numbers but also in consistent attendance. Kids just want to come back!"**

> **"Our church has never looked like this or felt like this before. It's just so cool!"**

> **"Just when they finally get Sunday school to be good, I have to leave—it's no fair!"**
> —a boy who was moving on to middle school

"Years ago when confirmands had to write their faith story, we'd get really sloppy short paragraphs about how their parents wanted them to get confirmed and be members. Now that the children have grown up in our new Sunday school using the multidimensional approach, they're writing two and three pages about their personal experiences with God and how they can see and feel God's hand in their lives. It's awesome!"
—*an elder in a Presbyterian Church*

"I don't think I ever really understood the Bible until I started teaching it this way. I think it's done more for my faith than it has for the kids!"
—*a dad/volunteer*

"One of our third grade boys cried when he had to miss Sunday school to go to a Kansas City Chiefs football game!"

The success of this model isn't difficult to understand. *We're teaching kids the way God made them to learn!* Let's take a look at what research and educational theory have taught us about how God made kids.

Pathways to a Child's Mind

Thinking in terms of children, how would you define "smart"? Since the development of IQ tests in the early 1900s, we've been trained to think of smart in terms of verbal, logistical and math abilities. These abilities are easy to measure in standardized tests, and for decades those tests have dictated whether children will be selected to participate in programs for the "gifted," or if expectations will be for average or below average schoolwork. The dismaying fact is that these expectations tend to become self-fulfilling prophecies: kids tend to perform up to teachers' expectations.

Being involved with children quickly opens our eyes to the great variety of ways God gifts people. The halting reader exhibits great skill on the playground. Some children excel at organizing games, while others work meticulously on expressive pieces of art. Some who are shy in conversation may bloom in a role onstage. Some demonstrate intrinsic knowledge of how to involve a child who is feeling left out. Verbal and math skills indeed! God makes each child "smart" in diverse and unique ways.

In 1983, Howard Gardner, educational research professor at Harvard Graduate School of Education, published a brilliant theory of how people learn and respond to their environment. His thinking revolutionized teaching and gave many of us a new understanding of ourselves and the children we work with. Gardner presented the idea that each person possesses several "intelligences." He began with seven intelligences. A few years later the list grew to eight. Here are Gardner's eight basic intelligences, followed by my personal explanations.[i]

 **LINGUISTIC-VERBAL**—the capacity to use words effectively, orally or in writing.

We speak of people who have a preference for this intelligence as being "word smart." You will notice that some of your students love to talk, do word searches, read and play with words. Some can be disruptive by always having to chat even when you are telling a story. *On the flip side,* some of your students need to read the words in order to understand the story more fully; they may be more quiet. Both types of students may have a strong linguistic-verbal preference.

To encourage the development of this intelligence in all your students, use activities such as storytelling, large and small group discussions and brainstorming, books and worksheets, manuals, writing activities, word games, sharing time, student speeches, talking books and cassettes, extemporaneous speaking, debates, journal keeping, choral reading, individualized reading, memorizing linguistic facts, tape recording their words, using word processors, publishing, writing dramas, newscasts, slogans, bumper stickers, imaginary diaries, songs, graffiti walls, advertisements, letters, sequels, interviews, crossword puzzles and poetry.

 **LOGICAL-MATHEMATICAL**—the capacity to use numbers effectively and to reason well. This includes sensitivity to logical patterns and relationships.

We refer to this intelligence with children by saying that they have the ability to be "math smart." You will notice that some of your students have as their preference reasoning skills and interest in putting things into logical sequences.

To encourage the development of this intelligence in all your students, be sure to include activities such logical puzzles, codes, sequencing, outlining, math problems, syllogisms, analogies, patterns in data, measurements, averages, percentages, graphs, science thinking, timelines, strategy games and categorizing facts.

 **SPATIAL**—the ability to perceive the visual-spatial world accurately and to perform transformations upon those perceptions. It includes the capacity to visualize and graphically represent visual or spatial ideas.

We refer to this intelligence as "picture smart." You may notice that children who have this intelligence as one of their preferences may close their eyes while you tell the story so that they can picture it in their minds. *On the flip side,* other students who are "high picture people" may actually be distracted by all of the visual stimuli in the room.

To encourage the development of this intelligence in all your students, utilize these kinds of techniques in your lessons: charts, graphs, diagrams, maps, photography, videos, visual puzzles, mazes, 3-D construction kits, art appreciation, imaginative storytelling, picture metaphors, creative daydreaming, painting, jigsaw puzzles, sculptures, visual outlines, mind mapping, board games, card games, architecture, visual thinking exercises, computer graphics software, optical illusions, telescopes, microscopes, picture literacy and more!

BODILY-KINESTHETIC—the capacity to use one's whole body to express ideas and feelings and the facility to use one's hands to produce or transform things.

We refer to this intelligence as "body smart." You'll notice children who just can't sit still, or who "travel" while speaking to you. Some constantly fiddle with their hands. We need to allow these children to move as they learn. They will actually retain information better if we let them move than if we insist they sit still. *On the flip side,* having a higher level of "body smarts" could also manifest itself in the small motor skills that coordinate with doing artwork, so it's important to remember that these intelligences are blended in each of us.

To encourage the development of this intelligence in all your students, be sure to incorporate these things into your lessons: creative movement, field trips, mime, crafts, body maps, cooking, gardening, manipulatives, virtual reality software, sign language, body language (charades), active games, echo pantomime, dance, large floor games, scavenger hunts and the like.

MUSICAL—the capacity to perceive, discriminate, transform, and express musical forms.

We refer to this intelligence as "music smart." This particular intelligence is often misunderstood, or translated as having a musical talent. What we're really talking about is the ability we all have to learn through music. Music and sound are around us every day and are not limited to singing or instrumentation. Church school teachers who insist that all the children sing a song or join the children's choir misunderstand the musical intelligence.

It's better is to find ways to use music to enhance the teaching environment, to set a mood, to interpret the story and to find ways to encourage this intelligence in all the children. Those children who have this as a preference *may* have the ability to sing, but that is not always the case. *On the flip side,* some children who have a high musical intelligence may actually be distracted by too many noises in the learning environment. On a personal note, since this is one of my (Mickie's) preferences, I find that I cannot work and listen to vocal music at the same time. I have to stop and sing along with everything! Even some deeply moving instrumental music will distract me; as the music takes hold, my imagination starts to run away with me. So be careful with this one. Don't assume that a child who can't sing is low musically, or that a child who does sing functions well with a constant stream of music.

To encourage the development of this intelligence in all your students, sing songs, tap fingers, listen for sounds, play musical instruments, listen to mood music, play CDs as background music for other projects, identify a type of music with a Bible story, hunt for music in the sounds around us.

 **INTERPERSONAL/RELATIONAL**—the ability to perceive and make distinctions in the moods, intentions, motivations and feelings of other people. Sensitivity to facial expressions, voice and gestures.

We refer to this intelligence as "people smart." Children with a high preference in this intelligence may be the ones who love group work. *On the flip side,* they may be the children who are so in tune with the moods around them that they are hesitant to speak up. They may be overwhelmed by someone else's insensitivity and keep to themselves.

To encourage the development of this intelligence in all your students, use these strategies: group games, cooperative projects, discussion groups, tasks with partners, board games, collaborative learning, community service projects, parties and allowing kids to take turns leading.

INTRAPERSONAL/INTROSPECTIVE—the ability to act adaptively on the basis of self-knowledge. Being aware of one's inner moods, intentions, motivations and a capacity for self-understanding.

We refer to this intelligence as "self smart." Children with a strong preference in this intelligence are likely to be reflective and quick to experience "ah-ha!" moments in their learning. These children tend to have a high sense of wonder which gives them an extraordinary pathway for experiencing God.

To encourage the development of this intelligence in all your students, try these kinds of activities: keeping a diary, praying, silent reflection, guided meditation, daydreaming, independent study, self-paced instruction, one-minute reflection periods and individualized projects and games.

NATURALISTIC—the attraction to and skill with plants, animals, natural phenomena and the environment. We refer to this intelligence as "nature smart." Children with a high preference in this intelligence love being outdoors—and frankly, what child doesn't?

To encourage the development of this intelligence in all your students, have them go on nature hikes, classify plants, feed animals and grow plants. Since God is the God of creation, this should be easy!

The most important thing to remember about these intelligences is that we all have them all. We need to be careful not to put people in boxes by using phrases like "You are a linguistic-verbal person" or "You must be logical/mathematical." Instead we need to encourage the development of *all* the intelligences in everyone and tap into their power to capture information for long-term retention and transformation.

Think for a moment about the complex ways the intelligences work together. A child playing a ball game needs bodily-kinestheic intelligence to run, kick and catch, spatial intelligence to become orient-ed to the playing field and to anticipate the trajectories of balls, and lin-guistic and interpersonal intelligences to successfully argue a point or shout out instructions to teammates.[iii] (Armstrong, 1994).

As you've seen, these intelligences don't manifest themselves in any one particular fashion. Each person is a bundle of all of the intelligences in different proportions. A child who is quiet may be highly "linguistic-verbal" because reading is what she loves, while another child who is also highly "linguistic-verbal" may be loud and talkative but doesn't like to read. Make it your purpose to avoid "labeling" students with one particular intelligence; instead, look for the potential of all your students to develop all the intelligences so they can more fully experience the wonder of knowing God.

A Moving Example

Just recently I helped my parents move out of their home of 35 years. At the end of the move we found ourselves with the inevitable pile of stuff no one wanted, so we called someone to haul it away. When he pulled up in the driveway with one truck, I thought, "He's crazy if he thinks all of this stuff is going to fit in there!" Then, as I watched, an amazing thing happened.

He walked through the house and garage and picked certain pieces to be placed on the truck first. Gradually other items made it to the drive-way; he carefully placed item after item into the truck—just so! Amazingly everything fit like a glove. When he was almost done I asked, "Did you like to do puzzles as a child?" He stopped and said, "Why yes I did, I'd spend hours on puzzles. Why do you ask?" I had to laugh. Here was a man who was still doing puzzles—but for a living. Obviously, visual-spatial was one of his preferred intelligences, yet he couldn't do it without being highly bodily-kinesthetic and mathematical-logical! He was a perfect example of how multiple intelligences play themselves out in our lives.

How Do You Slice Your Pie?

God has given you and each of your students pathways for receiving his message of grace, salvation and love. Imagine a big pie (make it any kind you like!) cut into eight slices. Some slices are generous, others are not much more than a sliver. Each piece represents one of the eight intelligences.

The learning is on one side; God's Word is on the other. This would demonstrate that God's Word is going to come through all eight of these pie pieces (or pathways, as I call them) to penetrate the mind and heart of the student. One or more of these pathways might be particularly small because they are not the student's preferred intelligences.

Just imagine what would happen to the possibility of learning if those were the only intelligences we used to get God's message across!

This is how we have taught in the past. We have used only one or two intelligences, usually our own preferences, and missed our students almost entirely. Think of how God has created us—with all eight intelligences (and perhaps more as the research continues). Let's use them all! God's Word tells us to

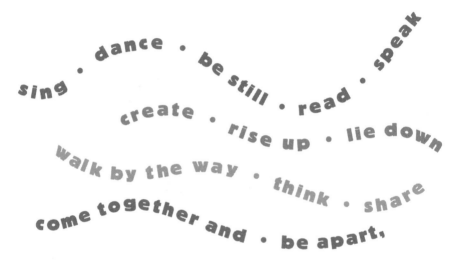

sing • dance • be still • read • speak
create • rise up • lie down
walk by the way • think • share
come together and • be apart,

in order to experience God and his grace. How we can do any less than use all of these pathways to convey God's message?

Finding Yourself

We all tend to teach the way we're most comfortable learning. That means you're going to need to stretch yourself to reach all your students. So take a moment to find yourself. This fun exercise will help you quickly identify your stronger intelligences.

The Shape of YOUR Mental Pathways Pie

A. _____ Spend time caring for pets and/or the plants you may have in your home or garden

B. _____ Hum, whistle, sing, play an instrument or listen to music

C. _____ Complete this numerical sequence and explain the logic:

45, _____ , 33, _____ , _____ , 15, _____

D. _____ Be with other people to do some kind of a group project or game or have a lively discussion in order to come to a consensus

E. _____ Do some activity that involves your entire body (running, swimming, dancing, etc.)

F. _____ Read, recall words once memorized, do word puzzles and/or listen to a lecture and remember what was said

G. _____ Remember a dream you had recently or spend time alone thinking

H. _____ Draw a quick picture of the floor plan of your home or draw a map to your friend's house; doodle or draw while explaining something

Read this list of activities lettered A-H. Rank these eight activities using the numbers 1 through 8, with 1 being your favorite and 8 being the thing you wish you never had to do. Rank each sentence with a different number. Don't think too deeply about it, just give it a go.

Now take a look to see how your "mental pathways pie" slices! You'll quickly see which intelligences are your strongest and which are areas that challenge you to stretch and grow. Here's how to interpret your preferences.

> **Letter A**—The Naturalistic Intelligence; Nature Smart
> **Letter B**—The Musical Intelligence; Music Smart
> **Letter C**—The Mathematical/Logical Intelligence; Math Smart
> **Letter D**—The Interpersonal Intelligence; People Smart
> **Letter E**—The Bodily/Kinesthetic Intelligence; Body Smart
> **Letter F**—The Verbal/Linguistic Intelligence; Word Smart
> **Letter G**—The Intrapersonal Intelligence; Self Smart
> **Letter H**—The Visual/Spatial Intelligence; Picture Smart

Take a look at your results. No surprises, were there? Understanding your own preferred intelligences gives you immediate insights into how your students may, in the words of Apple® computer ads, "think different."

Your Toolkit

God made kids all kinds of different ways, and they deserve the very best understanding of His Word we can give them! What does that mean when it comes to how you plan that special hour on Sunday morning? It means that storytelling is great, but it's not enough. Well-chosen games followed by thoughtful debriefing questions are fun and important, but they're just part of the picture. Music is a wonderful tool, because tunes and lyrics get inside kids' heads and stick—but some kids will gain more from it than others. As we teach kids God's Word, let's unpack the whole toolkit! Including Bible story-themed art, crafts, nature and science experiences, drama and food activities will enrich your kids' learning experiences and put to use all the pathways God has mapped into a child's mind.

Kids in their complexity are a wonderful reflection of their Creator. And it's our job to minister to the whole child. Intelligences are pathways to a child's mind. Our challenge is to provide a rich palette of learning experiences so that God becomes real, His love becomes tangible, and learning about Him is the high point of a child's week.

New Patterns for Leaders

For many years the pattern in Christian education has been read, discuss, write. That's great for kids who have "word smart" as their preference. But a class focused on reading, writing and discussion can be interminable for the child who has a "body smart" preference. She will squirm, wiggle, giggle and make a general nuisance of herself. If, however, that same child is discovering important insights about God's Word in a class that's full of lively activity, the lesson will be caught and it will stick.

Part of the genius of multidimensional learning is that it does not require a workshop leader to be all things to all kids. When we allow volunteers to teach according to their gifts (or dominant intelligence), teaching becomes a pleasure. You may have a "picture smart" person in your congregation who would quake at the notion of donning a costume and doing first-person storytelling. But leading kids in a workshop that focuses on an artistic response to a Bible story is a delightful prospect for your picture smart volunteer. Your workshop leaders teach what they most enjoy and their enthusiasm is contagious, both to the kids in their classes and other potential volunteers. In this way the multidimensional learning model contributes to the faith development of the children *and* the adults who work with them.

Edgar Dale's *Audio-Visual Methods in Teaching* (3rd ed., New York: Holt, Rinehart & Winston, 1969, p. 108) gives us these statistics about how we retain information.

We remember:
10% of what we read
20% of what we hear
30% of what we see,
50% of what we see and hear
70% of what we say
90% of what we say and do
100% of what we experience

These percentages show us very simply that we need to present the biblical story so that our children and their adult leaders *say, do and experience*. Using the full toolkit of intelligences brings a depth of experiential learning that makes your workshops/classrooms places of real life change.

A Simple overview

The Multidimensional Learning Environments model for Christian education helps churches:

+ *nurture children's faith development in rich learning environments that incorporate insights from ongoing brain research, and*

+ *motivate adult volunteers to deepen their faith walk and discover the joy of serving others by responding to opportunities for gift-based ministry.*

This new way of doing Sunday school is revitalizing Christian education programs across our nation. The paradigm shift involves moving from a contained classroom where one teacher presents a many-faceted lesson, covering a great deal of material quickly, to a series of theme-based rooms or workshops where kids approach a single Bible story in depth for a period of weeks. Workshop leaders repeat the lesson as groups of kids rotate from room to room each week. In this transformation,

✦ *Rooms become workshops—theme-based learning environments. Instead of having grade level classrooms, you may have a drama room, an art room, a computer room, a storytelling room, a movie room, a science and cooking lab and a map room. The choice and number of workshops is up to you.*

✦ *Adult volunteers teach workshops that flow from their personal giftedness and passion. They focus on the Bible story for an entire hour using one main learning medium. They prepare one lesson and teach it to rotating groups of children over a period of weeks.*

✦ *Groups of children rotate to different workshops each week, sampling a rich variety of learning experiences as they approach the Bible story from each of the intelligences.*

✦ *The entire group spends four to five weeks on a single Bible story, approaching it in a series of different modalities that allow the Bible truth to sink and take root in children's minds and hearts. We make the conscious choice to pull Sunday school out of fast forward and allow time for children to process, test and apply what they've learned.*

✦ *Creative people from the congregation combine their skills and vision to create interior design themes for the children's ministry area. Murals transform walls and hallways into authentic-look-ing Bible time environments. Tents, clay pots and oriental rugs create an inn-like setting that welcomes kids to the storytelling room. Shelves of well-organized art materials, work tables and display walls invite kids to an art workshop. A video room features darkened walls, comfy seating, large screen and a popcorn machine. A drama room centers around a roomy stage; boxes of costumes and props wait for young actors to bring a Bible story to life. Adults who contribute to this design work feel an incredible connection to the children's ministry that takes place there. Children feel valued when they see what the adults in the congregation have put into creating these enriched learning environments. They can't wait to dive in to the exciting learning that's about to unfold in these imagina-tion-stirring rooms.*

With these elements in place, your Sunday school moves to a rotation schedule that looks something like this.

	Sunday 1	Sunday 2	Sunday 3	Sunday 4	Sunday 5
Grade 1	AudioVisual	Storytelling	Art	Drama	Computer
Grade 2	Computer	AudioVisual	Storytelling	Art	Drama
Grade 3	Drama	Computer	AudioVisual	Storytelling	Art
Grade 4	Art	Drama	Computer	AudioVisual	Storytelling
Grade 5	Storytelling	Art	Drama	Computer	AudioVisual

The rooms listed in the chart above are examples of workshops church-es may choose. Every church is unique and will create workshops that make the best use of the giftedness of their adult volunteers and the physical space available. A drama workshop may sound exciting, but if a church has no one with drama skills and no available space to utilize drama as a teaching tool, it's best to make a different choice for its repertoire of workshops. That sounds like common sense, but sometimes seeing or hearing about a particular workshop in another place can cause churches to forget the importance of a serious assessment of their own situation.

You don't need to have all the finest, fanciest workshops to give your kids a wonderful learning experience. With God's help, you can create a marvelous program by making the best of what you *do* have.

The Shepherds' Role

One of the key roles in making this new model of Sunday school a success is that of the shepherd. Each age group (or mixed age grouping) needs one or two shepherds who commit themselves to the nurture and care of the group. In some churches shepherds have little or no preparation. They simply meet the children as they arrive and act as an extra set of hands in the workshops their group visits. Shepherds make it a point to get to know each of the children in their groups on a deeper personal level.

Shepherds also take responsibility for summarizing what the children have experienced that day, refreshing their memories from week to week and helping with their faith journals. They also can be asked to work on Bible verse memory, send notes and emails during the week, remember birthdays and contact kids who've been absent.

Shepherds provide the continuity that we so dearly miss in today's rushed society. Their purpose is to focus on the kids, pray for them, nurture them and provide a welcoming, caring presence each week.

In some rotation model churches, shepherds play an even greater role. In Vickie Bare's "Workshop Zone™" curriculum, available from Cook Communications Ministries, shepherds are the key disciplers of children. They meet with their groups for the first twenty minutes of each week before the kids move on to workshop activities. In this twenty minutes the shepherds work on specifics of kids' faith development: learning key scriptures, worshiping and praying together, and developing a sensitivity to missions.

Shepherds at Christ Church of Oakbrook where Vickie is Director of Christian Education often become so attached to their children that they stay with the same group until that group moves into the middle school ministry. Because these shepherds share their enthusiasm for their role with other adults, they end up recruiting new volunteers to join the Sunday school staff. Shepherds make the kind of heart connection with kids that their name implies.

Your Staff

To summarize, the multidimensional learning model functions with three distinct staff roles.

■ Director

The director sets the vision for the program, recruits and trains staff, chooses curriculum, troubleshoots and fills in when needed. This is a very involved, hands-on position. The director greets and directs kids before and after workshops and "floats" in the halls to check on workshops in progress. He or she is the point at which all aspects of the program intersect. You'll find a wonderfully detailed look at the director's role in Chapter 6.

■ Workshop Leaders

Specific environment leaders have the privilege of doing one lesson over a four to five week period as new groups of children rotate to their workshops. They teach in a setting that fits their particular giftedness and interest. In an ideal set-up, workshop leaders provide a review of the Bible story at the beginning of their activity time, then debrief the activity at the close of the session with thought-provoking questions that challenge kids to determine how the Bible truth will impact their lives in the coming week.

■ Shepherds

Shepherds are the nurturers of the program, attached to a specific group of children. They meet and accompany their group to their workshops and focus on developing personal relationships with kids in the group. Excellent programs involve shepherds in discipling children and looking to their faith development through prayer and Bible study.

The Wonderful Workshop Rooms

Churches typically have specific areas and rooms that are designated for children's ministry. These rooms are generally divided by class according to grade in school. In the multidimensional model, you transform the age-graded classroom into visually rich learning environments. As you prepare to implement this model in your church, don't feel that you need to create each of these workshops! You'll choose workshops based on the space you have available, the giftedness of your workshop leaders and the recommendations of the curriculum you choose.

There's something entirely wonderful about witnessing kids' reactions when they enter a creatively prepared workshop area for the first time. Eyes widen as the decor, murals and props transport them to another time and place. You can see their minds switch into the "let's go!" mode as they anticipate the fascinating activities that await them. Let's take a walk through several learning environments and note how each one offers a setting which appeals to particular combinations of the eight intelligences.

■ Storytelling Room

Modeling the oral tradition of the Hebrew people, kids sit around a "campfire" or at a cozy "inn" and hear a storyteller dressed in Bible time costume relate the Bible story from a personal perspective. Kids move on to a Bible story related project. For example, kids might listen to Moses and participate in the Passover Meal.

Intelligences: *intrapersonal, linguistic-verbal*

■ Bible Skills and Games Room

Kids hear and experience the Bible story through games, puzzles, quizzes, book searches, maps, newspapers, different translations of the Bible and Bible story books. For example, kids might actually be the game pieces as the floor becomes the game board for a quiz game about the Bible Story.

Intelligences: *linguistic-verbal, logical-mathematical, interpersonal*

■ Art Room

Kids respond to the message of the Bible story with personal art projects. The projects may stay in the workshop room to enhance the learning environment, be given to others, or go home with the kids. For example, kids might build Ten-Commandment Tablets by having each age group develop these tablets over the course of several weeks. The younger children do the shaping of the tablets out of Styrofoam®, the next grade uses wet cast material to wrap the tablets, the next age grade sands and paints the tablets and finally the older age group writes the words onto the tablets. Kids can make more than one set. They might make one in English and one in Hebrew to hang in the Sunday school area. All the children will remember that they contributed to their development. I (Mickie) did this with one of my first churches. The children gave me a set to keep when I left. These tattered tablets have a special place in my family room!

Intelligences: *visual-spatial, bodily-kinesthetic, inter-personal, logical-mathematical*

■ The Music/Movement Room

You won't find peace and quiet very often at this workshop! Kids raise their voices, play instruments and move their bodies in praise to the Lord. Some days children will be singing and playing authentic historical music or accompanying a story with music sound effects; sometimes they will be preparing for special musical productions to be shared. Children can listen to music tracks from popular video games and movies and imagine how they would weave the sounds into Bible story dramas. Many churches have found that Lycra® body-socks make wonderful props for children to wear as they act out Bible stories set to music.

Intelligences: *musical, bodily-kinesthetic, naturalistic, interpersonal*

■ Science and Cooking Lab

This workshop always generates a lot of excitement! Kids do food and hands-on science activities that allow them to explore the truth of the Bible story and its

application to their lives. For example, kids might do an experiment to understand the difference between change and conversion as we teach that Saul didn't just change his name to Paul—he was converted and transformed by the Holy Spirit into a new person. There's nothing quite as tantalizing as the aroma of bread baking. You might bring in a wheat mill and let children grind wheat or make bread on the quickest setting of a bread machine to experience the meaning of "I am the bread of life."
Intelligences: *visual-spatial, naturalistic, bodily-kinesthetic, interpersonal, logical-mathematical*

■ Computer Room

Kids play Bible computer games, use software to create their own Bible quizzes, research Bible topics and send emails to their adopted missionaries or pen pals in other churches.
Intelligences: *verbal-linguistic, bodily-kinesthetic, logical-mathematical, interpersonal, visual-spatial*

■ Drama/Puppetry Room

Children plan, act in and produce their own plays depicting the Bible story or a present-day response to the story. They may create TV news shows or interviews with Bible characters. Kids enjoy video taping and watching their performances. They can also write puppet shows, use all kinds of materials to make puppets and invent creative props to depict the story.
Intelligences: *linguistic-verbal, musical, bodily-kinesthetic, interpersonal, visual-spatial*

■ Audio/Visual Room

Children watch a video, film, filmstrips or puppet performance of the Bible story (and eat popcorn!). This workshop uses the *good* aspect of this medium to teach God's Word as opposed to how the world uses it. Leaders encourage kids to develop critical thinking skills to evaluate how the content aligns with biblical teaching. Responding to these theatrical images through writing in a journal allows children to reflect on what they are seeing and hearing.

Intelligences: *visual-spatial, intrapersonal, linguistic-verbal*

Note that all the workshops blend a collection of the intelligences. We do not have a "Musical Intelligences Room." The musical intelligence is stimulated in several different rooms. Within any one teaching rotation children need to use *all* the learning pathways in order to fully absorb and respond to the biblical message.

You will seldom use all the workshops in a unit or teaching rotation. For instance, if you have eight workshop rooms, a group of kids may visit four during one unit, then visit the other four during the following unit. Don't feel that you're required to create a multitude of architectural wonders! You can do a very effective rotation program with just a few workshop rooms.

Once you've chosen and set up your workshops, let the Bible story drive the activities in each room. When space is a constraint, create workshop rooms that do double duty. Art, Cooking and Science work well in the same room because access to storage cabinets, water, and a stove is important. Adding large maps can turn any room into a geography room. With a few basic workshops and the diversity of gifts your volunteers bring, you can "morph" learning environments to give the children in your ministry a rich variety of brain-tingling workshops.

Multiple Intelligences: Going Deeper

The effectiveness of the multiple intelligence approach to learning is no accident. It is a synthesis of brain research that goes beyond the swings in the educational pendulum that occur every few years.

■ Beyond Multisensory Learning

Not long ago the buzzword was "multisensory learning." Teachers were encouraged to use activities that included all five senses to knit new concepts into the fabric of a child's mind. This was a step in the right direction. But each intelligence, in fact, uses more than one sense. For example, there is not an auditory intelligence because you need the auditory sense to experience both music and linguistic-verbal. There is not a seeing intelligence because while our eyes are needed to see written words and pictures, all kinds of spatial experiences go beyond just what our eyes can see. Just giving children something to taste, touch, smell, hear and see does not mean that the learning is stimulating all eight pathways for learning.

■ Beyond Cognitive Learning Styles

The articulation of learning styles gave the educational community another tool in understanding how kids function. In the early days some referred to students as being either Visual Learners, Kinesthetic Learners or Auditory Learners, as if learning were one of these three. It was soon talked about as "See, Hear, Do." Later, theorists concluded that each person sees, hears and does, but has a preferred learning style he or she brings to the learning experience.

Cognitive learning styles gave us a clue about which intelligence a child prefers. But we do children a disservice when we allow them to operate only in their preferred learning style. Instead, we want to provide activities that stretch children's minds and allow for the development of all their intelligences. Leaning heavily on learning styles can put children in a restrictive mold. Kids will do their best learning when we challenge them to move beyond what's easy and comfortable into experiences that develop the whole person.

■ Beyond Learning Centers

One common reaction from people who hear about the Multidimensional Learning Model for the first time is, "Oh, it's just the old learning center approach." In fact, this model has moved well beyond that concept. With learning centers, each week children are allowed to choose the center where they want to work. Learning centers are designed to teach a different story or theme each week. The children decide how long they want to spend at each center, possibly visiting two or three centers within an hour. Many programs call for centers to be changed each week. With true Multidimensional Learning we guide the children beyond their comfortable preferences and give them in-depth learning experiences that encourage the development of all the intelligences. And workshops remain consistent in their set-up and teaching for four to five weeks.

The Multidimensional Learning Model builds on and refines each of these movements that have influenced education. By experiencing the biblical story in a variety of learning environments over four or five weeks, children receive the power of the story through all their intelligences. In this process, children retain, synthesize and act on what they've learned.

It's our goal to expose children to God's Word through environments that allow the biblical story to enter through all the "pathways" to a child's mind and heart.

When this process is nurtured and informed by God's Holy Spirit, we see the exciting result of children's lives being transformed into God's likeness. And that, after all, is our hope and our calling.

What You can Expect

The children in your ministry are growing up in a complex, post-modern world where truth is relative and individuals are their own ultimate authority. We need to equip the children entrusted to us with a sustaining understanding of our loving God as revealed in his Word. Multi-dimensional learning is a powerful tool for difficult times. When you embark on this learning adventure, you can expect

✦ *children fully engaged in challenging learning environments, eager to return and participate in new experiences*

✦ *each child developing a personal connection with a caring shepherd who is willing to give personal attention and nurture his or her spiritual formation*

✦ *a swell of volunteers who are enthusiastic about teaching the Bible through their areas of giftedness*

✦ *young lives being visibly transformed by the power of God's Word*

Joining the community of churches who have pioneered and refined this powerful approach to learning may be the most important step you take as a Christian educator. It's a challenging journey with eternal rewards. We want to share with you the store of knowledge we've accumulated over years of teaching children in this model so you'll have the confidence and expertise to take that step.

i The first seven definitions are drawn from *Multiple Intelligences in the Classroom* (Thomas Armstrong, ASCD, 1994). The description of Naturalistic intelligence is drawn from *The Complete MI Book* (Kagan & Kagan 1998).

ii Gardner, Howard. *Multiple Intelligences, the Theory in Practice,* Basic Books, 1993.

iii Armstrong, Thomas. *Multiple Intelligences in the Classroom,* ASCD, 2000.

2 Set the Stage

> "All who are skilled among you are to come and make everything the LORD has commanded."
> Exodus 35:10

Designing your children's ministry and setting up workshops for multidimensional learning are two of the most delightful challenges you'll ever tackle. Choosing a theme and bringing it to life with design, color, props and murals affords a wonderful opportunity to let your imagination roam. You get to think like a child again—and in so doing, set your heart on giving the kids in your ministry a place of wonder and delight where they will open the pages of God's Word and learn to know its Author.

From Tabernacle to Workshops

Making God's house a beautiful, inspiring place filled with the finest that artisans can contribute is a concept as old as the Book of Exodus. And we can find in the Book of Exodus inspiration and counsel for preparing a multidimensional learning environment today.

■ Detailed Planning

God is in the details! God gave Moses meticulous instructions for the building and equipping of the tabernacle. Look, for instance, at the instructions for a lampstand that was to be used to give light in the tabernacle.

> *Make a lampstand of pure gold and hammer it out, base and shaft; its flowerlike cups, buds and blossoms shall be of one piece with it. Six branches are to extend from the sides of the lampstand—three on one side and three on the other. Three cups shaped like almond flowers with buds and blossoms are to be on one branch, three on the next branch, and the same for all six branches extending from the lampstand. And on the lampstand there are to be four cups shaped like almond flowers with buds and blossoms. One bud shall be under the first pair of branches extending from the lampstand, a second bud under the second pair, and a third bud under the third pair— six branches in all. The buds and branches shall all be of one piece with the lampstand, hammered out of pure gold. Then make its seven lamps and set them up on it so that they light the space in front of it. Its wick trimmers and trays are to be of pure gold. A talent of pure gold is to be used for the lampstand and all these accessories.* — Exodus 25:31-39

Taking on the task of creating marvelous learning environments for your children involves thoughtful planning and attention to detail. Congregations that have done it say that kids' enthusiasm for learning God's Word is more than worth the weeks of ground work required to initiate the project.

■ Fine Craftsmanship

When God gave instructions for the construction of the tabernacle, He placed great emphasis on fine craftsmanship as well as gifting and designating individuals to take charge of the work.

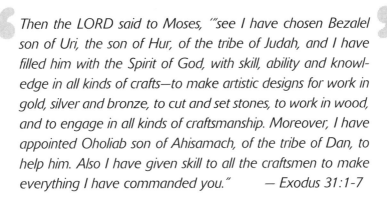

Then the LORD said to Moses, "'see I have chosen Bezalel son of Uri, the son of Hur, of the tribe of Judah, and I have filled him with the Spirit of God, with skill, ability and knowledge in all kinds of crafts—to make artistic designs for work in gold, silver and bronze, to cut and set stones, to work in wood, and to engage in all kinds of craftsmanship. Moreover, I have appointed Oholiab son of Ahisamach, of the tribe of Dan, to help him. Also I have given skill to all the craftsmen to make everything I have commanded you."   *— Exodus 31:1-7*

There are gifted people in your congregation who would take great delight in contributing to a project that will make such an impact on the spiritual growth of children. You may not know who they are yet, but God does! Listening in at rotation model conferences, you will hear varied and interesting stories of people God has used to make wonderful workshop rooms happen—from gifted high school students to an architect seeking a new calling. Many of these people had previous involvement in children's ministry. If God puts the job on your heart, He will bring forward people gifted to accomplish it! Start praying and searching, confident that there is no shortage of untapped talent among God's people.

Memories and Place

Can you see yourself in this picture? You're in the kitchen. You walk to the bedroom to get something. When you get to the bedroom, you haven't the vaguest notion what sent you there. What in the world were you going to fetch? You look around, but nothing clicks. So what do you do? *You walk back to the kitchen.* Back in the kitchen you pause and look around. Oh, yeah! The floor is cold and you need your slippers.

There is powerful truth in this little scenario that will help you understand the importance of creating distinct *places* where children learn. Our memories are indelibly tied to place.

You walk into a place you've not visited since you were young and what overwhelms you? Memories! Perhaps you've experienced a particularly close encounter with God at a particular place—your special private spot at a retreat center, a grassy place at the curve of a stream, in the corner booth of a restaurant, in a library cubby, or even—of all places—at church! Returning to that spot inevitably triggers memories of your experience and allows you to revisit that significant moment in your faith life.

Sounds and smells spark similarly vivid flashbacks. You know that if you've recently been affected by a serious traffic accident. The wail of a siren in the distance can make shivers run up and down your spine. The mouth-watering aroma of turkey in the oven always brings a little wave of nostalgia with mental slides of holiday gatherings when you crammed loved ones around groaning tables and ate until you were silly.

So, are special *places* where kids make fun *sounds* to accompany Bible stories and whiff the tantalizing *smell* of popcorn in the video workshop important in embedding faith-learning experiences in the minds of kids? Do they make a difference? Will the memories triggered by places, sounds and smells be as dynamic in the minds of children as they are in your mind? Oh, yeah. You bet. BIG TIME!

That, my friends, is precisely why we invest thought, time and resources to set the stage for kids' Bible learning experiences. We're using what we understand of our marvelous, intricate minds to allow God to plant indelible memories that will impact the lives of kids far beyond their Sunday school years.

Think of...

+ *a cozy loft where children snuggle on big floor pillows to talk privately with God or write and draw in faith journals*

+ *a slimy, disgusting blob of goo that's just as gross as sin and can't be removed without help*

+ *a large open room reverberating with scary, thumping music that invites kids to dramatize the wild chase scene across the Red Sea with soldiers in chariots in hot pursuit of Israelites fleeing on foot*

+ *a sea of brightly colored scarves waving in the air as kids dance and jump until they're breathless to celebrate God's love*

**These are tools—powerful tools
that God can use to build
unforgettable faith experiences
into the lives of children.**

This is why we set the stage. It's worth every moment of planning, every whack of the hammer, every brush stroke, every cent.

The Theme's the Thing

What will you call your new educational ministry? It's vitally important to choose a name that ties into the mission and ministry of your church. When you present the concept of this new model for children's ministry, you want everyone to feel that it's an integral part of your church's larger vision for ministry to the community. For instance, a church that sits at a five-corner intersection named their Sunday school "Crossroads." You can easily imagine how that name plays into a spiritual theme. University Christian Church in Fort Worth, Texas tells people that they want to be the church that "Joins You in Your Spiritual Journey." Therefore, their Sunday School is now called "Journey Land."

At St. Luke's United Methodist Church in Oklahoma City they have designed their ministry to be "The Great Adventure." Their hallways are painted to make you feel as if you have stepped into a hot air balloon. As you walk along the hallway, the murals look as if you are high up in the air looking down. At this church the senior pastor is also a pilot. For fun, the design team has painted tiny little images of his Piper aircraft in various spots. As if they were poring over a "Where's Waldo" page, kids enjoy finding the airplane.

One Methodist church in Texas decided to celebrate the history of John Wesley and Methodism as part of their theme. They've decorated their rooms to reflect the early American history of Methodist churches and the traveling of the itinerant preacher. Their rooms include an old school-house and a barn, complete with hay on the floor, hay bales for seating and corn stalks in the corner.

Churches whose ministry theme is "Growing in Faith" have used "Faith Forest" and "God's Garden" as the theme for their children's ministries.

There are hundreds of creative ways to weave your church's ministry theme into your new children's ministry concept. Let the theme represent everything you hope your children's ministry will be. Pray over every idea as you seek to coordinate the theme of your educational ministry with the overall mission of your church. This kind of thoughtful integration will smooth the way for the implementation of your program.

Gathering Ideas

If you know where to look, you can find a host of wonderful resources to inspire and coach you through the design and creation of your learning environment. Churches that use the rotation model are always excited about sharing what they've achieved. Check out these websites for a wealth of ideas.

+ *www.lordnking.com*
+ *www.churchschooldesign.com*
+ *www.sundaysoftware.com*
+ *www.jdbdirect.com*
+ *www.alassociates.com*
+ *www.emtweb.org*

Don't forget about Bible atlases and books about Bible lands. Maps, drawings and photographs will give you the details you need to flesh out workshops with a wonderfully authentic feel.

Lord and King Associates, Inc. offers a videotaped virtual tour of children's ministry areas in Chicago-area rotation churches. The video gives you a firsthand look at how nine churches of different sizes have creatively transformed their spaces with inspired themes and room designs.

Finally, you need to know about an incredible, must-have resource that will give you terrific ideas and tools for creating your workshop zone. Jan Hubbard, the nation's premier designer of workshops and children's ministry areas, has written a book titled, *Great Spaces, Learning Places*. In it she's compiled a wealth of information and advice that will set you confidently on the road to creating awesome environments for your Sunday school.

Jan has been involved in the multidimensional learning movement from the outset. In addition to her expertise as a noted interior designer, Jan has a great understanding of how environment impacts learning. *Great Spaces, Learning Places* addresses every aspect of designing your space: assessing your resources, getting your church on board, choosing colors and props and furniture and meeting building codes. She includes a primer on faux painting and a section on mural painting from professional muralist Dale Olsen. You'll see examples from several churches of the awesome learning environments Jan has created. *Great Spaces, Learning Places* is available from Cook Communications Ministries at 1-800-708-5550.

Avoiding Brick Walls

Committing to rotation-based multidimensional learning means making changes to the children's ministry area in your church building. Approval for changes comes through key committees who need to be fully vested in your plan before you begin.

I will never forget the time I ran into a brick wall. This particular brick wall was in the children's Sunday school area. It featured water stains, paint drippings and gouges in the mortar. It made sense to paint the wall a bright white so the colored tapestries we planned to use for area dividers would stand out. We approached the properties committee, not realizing that the simple matter of painting a wall could turn into a Pandora's Box. While we had received permission to change to this new model of ministry, our committee had not explained the full implications of upgrading the children's ministry area in the church building.

Changing to a new model of ministry is one thing. Touching a wall with paint is quite another! Some folks dug in their heels. Eventually I saw that if I gave up on painting the wall, I would gain permission to move ahead with other aspects of the project. So good things happened in the end. But I learned that laying careful groundwork with all the committees of the church goes a long way toward assuring a smooth road ahead.

I know of a wonderful church in the Midwest that built a magnificent new building with space specially designed for multidimensional/rotational children's ministry. Those who chose the paint colors for that area did not consult an interior design specialist, nor did they consider the impact color can have on people's attitudes and feelings. They painted the hallways in the entire church the same gold-brown flat paint. When I went to visit this church I was so appalled at the color that I found myself getting a headache. The children's ministry workers were beside themselves trying to find ways around this color, but it was clear that the wall color was non-negotiable. Furthermore, all props, posters and murals had to be taken down each week.

Not to be discouraged, this creative team of educators projected murals on the walls and set out rugs, fabrics and artificial trees each week to attain enriched learning environments. They did not allow skewed priorities to deter their commitment to multidimensional learning. Amazing things are happening in the lives of the children who attend there.

So take heart! You can do this—sometimes in spite of the powers that be.

Enhance—Don't Distract

Some well-meaning children's ministry directors who want to create a lively, energetic atmosphere for their kids make the mistake of filling every space with eye-popping colors and visually stimulating decor. This is an understandable but misguided approach.

Today's kids typically arrive at church in an over-stimulated state. They are accustomed to sensory overload from being bombarded with the fast-paced, in-your-face graphics that are typical of video games and TV programming. The last thing they need to see in a workshop where you want to promote quiet, reflective activities is a lime green wall with hot pink polka dots! In some workshops you'll want to use calming colors to create a quiet residential feel. On the other hand, screaming walls may be fine for a workshop where kids will play rowdy games and make lots of good noise.

As you think through the workshops you're going to offer, let their purpose dictate the ambience you'll create in those rooms. Consult an interior designer for help with what colors are best. There is an amazing amount of wonderful wallpaper and wallpaper murals available these days. Remember, you are creating an atmosphere for specific types of experiences, not just a cool room for one particular Bible story. And while design is important, always keep this in the front of your mind.

**Multidimensional learning is
ultimately not about the rooms,
but about what children do in the rooms.**

Prepare Your Wish List

List everything you could possibly want for your Sunday school remodeling and don't be afraid to ask for what seems impossible. Ask your team to dream and dream big—it's fun! In one church we called this the "Angel List," meaning that anyone who would give one or more of these items would then be considered an "Angel in the Kingdom." We put their names on an Angel List displayed in The Kingdom.

One children's ministry director recalled putting together a "Wish List" and asking for all kinds of things that would enhance the environments. She put "camel saddle" on her list, thinking how great it would look in the storytelling room. Colleagues wondered a bit at her sanity. Where in the middle of rural Wisconsin would one find such a thing? Imagine her delight when not one but two camel saddles were donated!

You never know what might show up if you ask. People who don't have the means or inclination to give a monetary gift may be quite willing to part with a treasure, knowing it will enhance the learning experiences of children in their church week after week.

One couple gave an unusual gift to the game room and teasingly say that it saved their marriage. Apparently, the husband had always wanted to build a full-size canoe. He did, and when it was finished he wanted to hang it over the mantel in their living room. Aghast at the idea of such an unwieldy piece of decor, the wife balked at the proposal. That's when the Wish List from the Sunday school ministry appeared and saved the day. Now this wonderful handmade canoe is proudly hanging on the wall in the Bible Skills and Game room, storing balls and ropes and nets and other assorted game items that are used each week at the church. Husband and wife are happy and the church is delighted to have such a wonderful accessory.

The Heart of the Giver

When you prepare your list, remember to ask for gifts given in love. When God gave Moses direction for the building of the tabernacle, He requested an outpouring of love from people who were grateful for their freedom and for God's ongoing provision. God told Moses to *ask* for offerings from "each man whose heart prompts him to give" (Exodus 25:2). Be prepared to receive and use what is prompted in the hearts of your people. You'll be amazed at what God prompts people to do.

Remember the fascinating items God included in the list for the tabernacle: "gold, silver and bronze; blue, purple and scarlet yarn and fine linen; goat hair; ram skins dyed red and hides of sea cows; acacia wood; olive oil for light; spices for the anointing oil and for the fragrant incense; and onyx stones and other gems" (Exodus 25:3-7). Look at the response!

> *All who were willing, men and women alike, came and brought gold jewelry of all kinds: brooches, earrings, rings and ornaments. They all presented their gold as a wave offering to the LORD. Everyone who had blue, purple or scarlet yarn or fine linen, or goat hair, ram skins dyed red or hides of sea cows brought them. Those presenting an offering of silver or bronze brought it as an offering to the LORD, and everyone who had acacia wood for any part of the work brought it. Every skilled woman spun with her hands and brought what she had spun—blue, purple or scarlet yarn or fine linen. And all the women who were willing and had the skill spun the goat hair. The leaders brought onyx stones and other gems to be mounted on the ephod and breastpiece. They also brought spices and olive oil for the light and for the anointing oil and for the fragrant incense. All the Israelite men and women who*

were willing brought to the LORD freewill offerings for all the work the LORD through Moses had commanded them to do.
— *Exodus 35:22-29*

The people of Israel continued to bring gifts "morning after morning" (Exodus 36:3) until Moses had to ask them to stop! If God provided so generously in the wilderness, think what He can provide through the people in your congregation who love Him and want the very best for His children. As you patiently and clearly share your vision of what God can do in the lives of children through these enriched learning environments, prayerfully ask God to inspire the giving that will make the program possible.

Generous Giving

Like any worthy project, creating multidimensional learning spaces requires financial resources. Imagine the task that God put before Moses: building and furnishing a beautiful place of worship from materials available in the middle of a vast, sparsely populated wilderness. No handy home improvement stores, credit cards or pickup trucks! Yet when it came to the building, there were materials in excess of what they could use. Now that's a God thing!

When a church dedicates itself to revitalizing its children's ministry, people come out of the woodwork to participate with their time, talents, money and possessions. People who are unable to work on the project physically often get caught up in the enthusiasm and decide to contribute financially. We find this phenomenon happening in churches all over the country. Nearly everyone prefers giving to a cause rather than an anonymous coffer. Make the educational ministry of your church a cause, and people will be interested in sharing ownership of it, whether through financial resources, Wish List resources, or time and talent. It can be very exciting!

What If I'm Not an Artist?

Not the artsy type? Never fear! There are talented people in your con-gregation who would love to get on board and help with this process. One of the wonderful things about transitioning to multidimensional learning is the way it brings people with gifts and abilities out of the woodwork.

Throughout history people have expressed their faith in God through art. Now is the time to unleash the dormant talents in your congrega-tion! There are artists out there just waiting to get involved. While they might not answer the call to be a "Sunday school teacher," they will be thrilled with the opportunity to contribute their artistic talent to creating a vibrant children's ministry area.

When I was introducing this concept in one particular church, I put out a newsletter notice asking for artists to come to a meeting. Only two people showed up, but they were both highly gifted and intrigued with the ideas I was sharing. Both worked diligently and faithfully creating the most wonderful of rooms (visit *www.cc-ob.org* to see some of the pictures).

Dale Olsen was an architect, but he'd always been fascinated by mural painting. I'll never forget the day he arrived to begin work on our first room. He arrived early with ladders, paint cans, canvas drop cloths, a portable radio, and even photographs of Israel. When I came with donuts in hand to encourage him, he turned to me and said "I was so excited to start this project that I could hardly sleep last night. I've been a Deacon, an Elder, an usher and served on the finance committee, but this is the first time I'm actually excited about doing something for my church because I'm finally using my true gift!"

One church tells the story of a young woman who volunteered to paint a mural. She was not a member of the church; she and her mother had recently moved to the area and were just starting to visit churches. Upon hearing of the need for artists this teenager stepped forward, submitted a sample of her work and was given permission to work on her own. Week after week she sat in that space painting the most beautiful scene of the Sea of Galilee. People stopped in to see her work; as time went by she and her mother felt more and more comfortable calling that church their home. Once when the minister of education stopped in, she asked this young woman why she would volunteer though she wasn't even a member. She said "My mom and I moved here right after my father died. He was an artist and I miss him. Painting this mural has helped me feel close to him again. It's like he's right here with me. Thank you for letting me do this."

Other churches have discovered the fun of "color by number." They use transparencies to project pre-drawn artwork onto the walls. The person in charge chooses numbered colors for various portions of the mural and pencils numbers into sections drawn on the wall. With brushes, paints and drop cloths set out on a worktable, people drop by and paint whenever they have time. Children, youth and adults work side by side. What fun! The ownership of those murals is quite broad; people take pride in knowing they had a hand in the work.

Some churches invite various adult education classes to adopt rooms or hallways and take charge of the design and decoration of the space. In one church in the Atlanta area I remember seeing an entire ceiling of tiles painted by different families, each with its own personality but all forming one unified theme.

One of my favorite stories comes from a church whose design team got so creative that they decided to carry their Egyptian theme into the restroom decor. They painted the walls with hieroglyphics and other artifacts that gave the feeling of stepping into the land of Moses. Then they hung a sign designating the area that said, "Let my people go." Either they had a great sense of humor, or they just got silly with overwork!

Be in prayer. Don't be in too much of a hurry to get something up on the walls. Ask God to call the people He has in mind to use their gifts. As the transformation takes place, you will see the blessing that comes from people using their giftedness to bring new life to your children's ministry.

Focus on What You Have

What's unique about your church and its people? Focusing on your congregation's unique qualities will help you create a children's ministry that will work beautifully in your situation. While you may find inspiration and ideas from what other rotation churches are doing, avoid a cookie cutter approach. God has gifted your people with particular gifts for your setting.

Multidimensional learning is not a program to ADOPT, but a paradigm to ADAPT.

Focus on what you have and make the most of it. If you have one large room instead of several smaller rooms, use that large room creatively. No matter what size church you are, you can do this. Sometimes people think that this model is only effective in large churches. In fact, this model was started in smaller churches in an effort to bring new life to an otherwise dwindling program.

Small Sunday school attendance is not always reflective of the size of the church building. If you have rooms that are sitting unused, your design team can get them back on line. There are several different ways to bring the rotational model to the small church. Let's look at how to over-come some of the challenges you may face.

■ Plan One

Perhaps your church has four rooms, each with a different learning environment. If you have small attendance and few volunteers, don't feel that you must use each room each week. Your rotation could look something like this.

	Sunday 1	Sunday 2	Sunday 3	Sunday 4
Grades 1-2	AudioVisual	Computer	Art	Drama
Grades 3-5	Computer	AudioVisual	Drama	Art

■ Plan Two

Some churches have a nice group of children, but only one large space to work with. Make the rotation model work by dividing the room into four sections or corners. Place a tent in one corner for storytelling and drama. Put a table and chairs in another corner for art and science. Put a TV/VCR and pillows (or carpet squares) in another corner. Set up the fourth corner with games and Bibles. Again, you can use all four corners each week, or just two or three at a time.

■ Plan Three

An outside-the-box approach involves moving workshops away from the previously designated children's ministry area to other spaces in the church. For example, use "Worship" as one of the workshops and have the children attend the opening part of the worship service; use the church kitchen as the Cooking Workshop; use large storage areas as quiet storytelling places; make use of out-of-the-way hallways for games and movement. You might want to keep these "workshop rooms" a secret, so discovering what's happening where will be an adventure for the kids from week to week.

■ Plan Four

For the church that only has one room and a small group of children, the answer is simple! Each week the room becomes a different environment. You do *not* need to decorate elaborately each week. Instead, concentrate on a different experience with the Bible story. Enhanced environments are wonderful, but they are not the central focus of this model. What's important is the variety of ways children encounter the Bible story. For this particular situation, the rotation model looks like this.

All the Children	Experience
Week 1	AudioVisual
Week 2	Computer
Week 3	Drama
Week 4	Art
Week 5	Storytelling

Shared Space

With shared space, many church educators have learned to become "quick change artists" and have found ways to convert rooms into learning environments via rolling dividers, curtain material, carpet squares and artificial plants. Extension rods and fabric make for a quick stage, and a pup tent makes a great storytelling center. These are things that can move in and out quite easily. Use rolling drawers for art supplies to move in an out of your art workshop area.

If you happen to share rooms with a daycare center or preschool, make arrangements to share storage bins. Some rolling dividers are used in preschools as bulletin boards. Designate one side of the bulletin board divider for the preschool and the other side for the Sunday school. Turning these dividers around is a quick, easy way to switch the environment.

In her book, *Great Spaces, Learning Places,* Jan Hubbard offers several strategies for using shared space effectively. Her business, Design Directions for Church School, also offers detailed plans for building rolling art storage, market carts and other space solutions such as lofts and portable drama walls.

**With shared space,
many church educators
have learned to become
"quick change artists"**

The Large Church

The rotation model adapts beautifully to large churches. If you have more than four or five classes for all your children, here are a couple of ways to manage the rotations.

■ Large Church Option One

Create two of each learning environment. For example, design two art rooms, two game rooms, two storytelling centers, etc. Rotate your classes with lower grades through one set of rooms while the older grades rotate through the other set. While this takes some planning, it does simplify the material, as you will be able to gear each set of workshops to a more specific age span. Vickie Bare's *Workshop Zone*® rotation curriculum is set up in this manner, with separate workshop tracks for older and younger kids. Matching teachers with specialties in either younger or older grades works well with this model.

■ Large Church Option Two

Create eight to ten learning environments. Rotate half the children through workshops one through four while the other half of the children go through workshops five through eight for the first story rotation. Then have the children go to the opposite set of workshops during the second story rotation. The rotation schedule looks something like the chart on p. 71.

■ Large Church Option Three

If you have large rooms but not many of them, consider having each room function as a dual workshop. Set up half of the room for one activity and half of the room for another. From one week to the next, groups of children can simply switch sides of the room.

	Week 1 Creation	Week 2 Creation	Week 3 Creation	Week 4 Creation
Grade 1A	Video	Storytelling	Art	Drama
Grade 1B	Cooking	Video	Storytelling	Art
Grade 2A	Bible Games	Cooking	Video	Storytelling
Grade 2B	Puppetry	Bible Games	Cooking	Video
Grade 3A	Computer	Puppetry	Bible Games	Cooking
Grade 3B	Drama	Computer	Puppetry	Bible Games
Grade 4A	Art	Drama	Computer	Puppetry
Grade 4B	Storytelling	Art	Drama	Computer

	Week 1 Joseph	Week 2 Joseph	Week 3 Joseph	Week 4 Joseph
Grade 1A	Computer	Puppetry	Bible Games	Cooking
Grade 1B	Drama	Computer	Puppetry	Bible Games
Grade 2A	Art	Drama	Computer	Puppetry
Grade 2B	Storytelling	Art	Drama	Computer
Grade 3A	Video	Storytelling	Art	Drama
Grade 3B	Cooking	Video	Storytelling	Art
Grade 4A	Bible Games	Cooking	Video	Storytelling
Grade 4B	Puppetry	Bible Games	Cooking	Video

Your Church, Your Way

The rotation model is just that—a model. It's flexible enough to adapt to any imaginable church situation. Allow the personality and physical situation of your church to shape the look and design of your learning environments. The heart of the model is creating a gift-based ministry in which volunteers teach from their strengths and lead children through life-changing encounters with God's Word. Gorgeous workshops are a tool, not a prerequisite.

K.I.S.S.

We'll define that acronym as "Keep It Simple, Sweetie." Perhaps you've visited a church with incredible learning environments and you're ready to try to build Rome in a day. Don't! *Small improvements can bring big rewards.* Temper enthusiasm with reality. Don't worry about having every room perfectly appointed before you begin. Take your time. Develop your themes and your design. Let the children help you make the changes. Nothing promotes buy-in like personal involvement. Take what you have, like the loaves and fishes, bring them to the Lord and let God multiply the results. Be faithful in the little things and watch what God does!

I recently heard from an educator who was tremendously excited about what this new concept was doing for her church. Her voice was filled with enthusiasm as she exclaimed to me on the phone "We are just starting this and in less than a month we went from having only three children in Sunday school to having forty!" Having three children to begin with meant that this dear teacher was not working with expansive space, state-of-the-art workshops or dazzling hallways. She simply started teaching the wonderful stories of Scripture with experiences that appealed to all the intelligences. Word spread and the children came!

Trust God

Above all, trust the Lord to bring about His plan for your children's ministry. I know of a church that was eager to move to the rotation model in their Sunday school. They clearly felt God's direction. However, one lady in the church strongly opposed the change. A group of moms met to pray about the issue. I counseled them to take their time and keep praying. They prayed specifically for the lady who opposed the change. She had always been involved in Sunday school and wanted to see the ministry stay the same.

The moms prayed for wisdom and grace. One by one, others in the church came forward to ask the pastor for a more innovative Sunday school for their children. The mothers in the prayer group grew closer to each other and realized that God had softened their hearts toward the woman whose opposition frustrated them. Out of the blue one day, the woman resigned from leadership. Not out of frustration or anger, but because her daughter was going to have a baby and she wanted to be available to help. In God's good time, the congregation eagerly moved to the rotation model without any bad feelings. God's timing is perfect.

Many churches have accomplished the move to the rotation model without any paid staff for Christian education. Volunteers accomplished all the planning and redesign. The stories they tell of relationships being built along with the rooms are heartwarming.

"See I am doing a new thing,"
the Lord says in Isaiah 43:19.

How do you usher in God's new thing? Understand the whys.

**Plan prayerfully.
Communicate with passion
and compassion.**

Ask God to prompt joyful giving. Unleash the hidden talent in your congregation. Focus on and use what you have. Adapt, adapt, adapt. Don't worry about being perfect. Then stand back and applaud as God does a "new thing" in your church!

The Heart of the Matter

Delightful rooms, eye-catching murals and perfectly chosen props do not a children's ministry program make.

Having devoted an entire chapter to principles of creating learning environments that captivate children and stimulate their intelligences, it's time to balance the equation. Delightful rooms, eye-catching murals and perfectly chosen props do not a children's ministry program make. You can top out the budget creating workshops that wow but still fall short of your calling: giving kids a real-life understanding of what it means to know Jesus and be His disciple. Enriched learning environments are valuable tools, and they certainly draw the interest and enthusiasm of the kids. But the heart of the matter is this:

**It's not the rooms—
it's what happens in
the rooms.**

What Katie Learned

One of my (Vickie's) favorite parts of Sunday morning is what happens after the kids have been released from their workshops. Armed with a basket full of stickers, gummi bears, matchbox cars and other treasures, I take my post in the hallway at Kid Central. By the time I arrive, there is usually a crowd of kids eager to tell me what they heard, cooked (and ate), or how their science experiment made a mess or changed into goo or was generally the grossest and coolest thing they ever saw.

This hallway ministry serves at least two purposes: it gives me the opportunity to stay connected to the kids as I hear their lives "speak" by what they say or don't say, and by what they choose to tell me about Sunday school. It also helps me discern if the lessons and activities that they are participating in are sowing the seeds of life-change that I've been commissioned to plant.

I'll never forget a little girl named Katie who came to see me every week after Sunday school. Katie was in kindergarten, but she was wise beyond her years. She knew the Bible story for each lesson and could usually quote her memory verse perfectly. One cold December morning, Katie began to tell me the familiar story of how baby Jesus was born in a stable and was visited by shepherds. Something in the way Katie was telling me the story made me realize that she didn't really understand how wonderful this birthday was.

"Katie," I said, "who is Jesus?" A long, quiet pause followed while she stared down at her shoes. Katie wasn't used to getting things "wrong," you see.

"Jesus is our Savior," she replied.

"That's right. But do you know what else?" I asked. "Jesus is God. He came down from heaven and was born as a baby so He could save you from your sins."

"Why?" she almost whispered.

"Because He looked down through the ages and saw many people He loved, and one of them would be named Katie, and He wanted her to live in heaven with Him one day." Just then her older brother came up to join Katie.

"You know what, Jamie?" Katie asked. "Jesus is God and I'm going to live with Him in heaven some day."

With tears in my eyes, I looked up to see Katie's mom's sniffling into a tissue. I just know that all over heaven angels were giving each other high fives because Jesus had become more real and wonderful than ever to a little girl named Katie.

What's Good and What's Best?

Experiences like the one I had with Katie are at the heart of everything we do. We want kids to understand how precious they are to God and to know Jesus as a friend and as their savior. How do we get to those moments?

Let's look at a list of good things that you want to happen in a workshop room. Gnaw on the list for a few moments, then identify your top four priorities.

____ Kids become a community of disciples.

____ Kids learn their way around the Bible.

____ Kids discover the life-application of their Bible memory verse.

____ Kids are taught by well-informed, passionate leaders.

____ Kids engage in fresh, challenging activities.

____ Kids learn Bible truths.

____ Kids have fun and want to come back.

____ Kids develop a personal faith in Jesus.

____ Kids apply the basic tenets of the Christian faith in their lives.

____ Kids share concerns and pray together.

____ Kids are mentored by caring adults.

____ Kids practice the disciplines of Christian discipleship.

____ Kids grow in their understanding of who God is.

**Was choosing your top four more
difficult than you first thought?
Well, it should be!**

We want all those good things to happen in our workshops. But we need to sift through the good to get to the best, then make sure that the best gets addressed in every workshop, every week.

The Long View

When you plan or choose your curriculum, it's so important to keep the long view in mind. It's easy to be caught up in choosing exciting work-shop activities and let the bigger picture fade with the tyranny of the urgent. Don't do it. Devote yourself to setting long-term goals that will define everything else that happens in your ministry.

When children finish fifth grade and move on from your ministry, what do you hope will be written on their hearts?

Here are the goals we've set for our ministry at Christ Church of Oakbrook.

KIDS WILL

Confess Jesus Christ as their personal Savior

Celebrate who God is as they worship

Commit to following Christ's example
with their behavior and attitudes

✻

Convey the love of God in their relationships
and interactions with the world

✻

Cultivate their prayer voice

✻

Catalyze change in the world by
becoming "missions-minded"

✻

Connect with God's Word as their
"instruction manual for life"

✻

Contribute to the Body of Christ
through their time, gifts and talents

Are you thinking we have high expectations? Sometimes we think that too! But let me invite you to join me at a special service on a Sunday afternoon in June. This is the day we celebrate the 5th graders who have completed their sojourn in our children's ministry program and are ready to pass into the care of the middle school leaders.

It never fails. Every time my fifth graders graduate into middle school, I get a little choked up. This year would be no different. As Josh Higgins (our middle school director) and I greeted the fifth graders and welcomed the parents to our annual Fifth Grade Devotional service, different scenes from the lives of these kids came to memory.

I thought about how Rachel's mom had called me to tell me the "life verse" that Rachel had chosen when she received her third grade Bible two years earlier. "Vickie," she said, "she knew exactly which verse she wanted. When I asked her she told me she wanted the last part of Matthew 28:20, when Jesus tells His disciples 'I will be with you always.'" God's Word had impacted Rachel. Today she was moving on.

Then there was Dominic. Always a gentleman, always willing to help me with anything I asked. And Lindsey, who wrote a faith-filled note of encouragement to me when I was going through chemotherapy. That note is still in my Bible. What a privilege to know I helped plant the seeds that God made grow!

The service began with prayer and a brief word from Josh to the kids. Then both Josh and I shared the different ways we had experienced a quiet time with God. When it came time to present the devotional book we had selected to help the kids establish a daily quiet time, the shepherds from each class came forward to read the faith statements that the kids had made weeks before. We had asked them to respond to the following question:

"What is the most important thing you could tell someone about Jesus?"

The answers were as diverse and special as the kids who wrote them. Meredith wrote, "The most important thing I could tell a friend about Jesus is that he didn't say, 'Look at me! I'm a King!' He was humble, and a serving person." MacKinzie said, "He can be your best friend." And Aaron reminded us, "You can trust Jesus, He will always be there." Elliott said, "He loves you." By the time we reached the end of the service and heard Jack's words about Jesus, there wasn't a dry eye in the house. "Jesus cares for you," Jack's statement read. "He cares about what things happen in your life. He cares about how you respond to others."

These proclamations were simple but they spoke volumes. In the years these kids had spent growing together as a community of faith, they had developed a personal and intimate knowledge of Jesus. Their Jesus is a friend who loves them deeply, who can be trusted, who is accessible even though he is the King of the Universe, who wants them to live a life of love, and who cares about the everyday, practical things in their lives.

You can imagine the overwhelming gratitude to God we feel when our kids respond with this kind of spiritual maturity, self-knowledge and God-given sense of purpose. It's humbling and amazing, and it assures us that God has blessed every ounce of effort we've put into building and refining our children's ministry.

The Colossal Concept

Which brings us to another colossal concept God has kept before me as I've developed the Workshop Zone™ curriculum.

**It's about transformation,
not information.**

You can pack kids' heads full of Bible verses and names of patriarchs, the Ten Commandments, the Fruit of the Spirit and the Armor of God. But that's just information (albeit the best information) until it hits the heart, knits itself into the fabric of kids' beings and surfaces in transformed lives.

It's a God-sized goal. Which means that, thankfully, we aren't expected to be more than the vessels that the Holy Spirit uses to initiate and expedite spiritual transformation. It is our job, however, to offer transformational opportunities as the essential core of our goals—goals that need to be clearly stated and reinforced week after week in our curriculum.

Teaching for Transformation

So how do we work toward life change? What elements do we include in the precious time we have with kids so they not only get Bible knowledge, but synthesize the information they've learned so they can take it to the streets and practice what they are learning in Sunday school? I offer the following basic (but not exhaustive) reflections.

▪ Begin by building relationships

The biblical model that Jesus gives us for making disciples is that of worship, growth and service in the context of relationship and community. For kids to feel the freedom to share their fears, their problems and their doubts as well as their victories, an environment of intimate trust must first exist.

A case in point: Valerie was a fourth grade girl whose father lost his job just after the New Year. Though she had lots of support at home, she was struggling with fear and the changes that were taking place in her household. Because her shepherd had intentionally become involved in the lives of the kids in her care, Val felt comfortable sharing her anxieties with her classmates. The kids responded to this trust by offering words of wisdom from their own experiences or reminding Val of God's faithfulness. One told her: "Val, remember when Peter sank? He stopped looking at Jesus. No matter what happens, you gotta look at Jesus."

■ Don't talk down to the kids

Every year I have one or two grown-ups who tell me something like, "The kids will never understand the concept of grace." When I first began writing rotation curriculum, I let all of these voices influence my decisions. But then I realized that we can put training wheels on theology and help kids begin to decipher deeper wisdom in God's Word. So, when I tell kids that grace means God is on their side, they get it.

During our Year of Grace, we played a ring-toss game that was impossible to win. I told the shepherds who were assisting with the lesson that every time a child threw a ring toward the target, they were to give the child M&M's™ and say how wonderful he or she was, even if the ring landed nowhere near the target. The first few times this happened the kids looked confused, but they didn't refuse the candy. When the game was over, I asked, "What did you think of that game? Wasn't it fun?"

Luke looked at me with his hands full of M&M's™ and said, "Miss Vickie, you need to take these back. I don't deserve them."

"Why, Luke?" I asked.

"I didn't hit the target one time!" he said. Could I have asked for a better segue to talk to second graders about grace?

▣ Speak into the lives of the kids in your ministry

The kids who have been entrusted into our care live in a world as full of joy and opportunity as it is beset by brokenness, hurry, stress and heavy burdens. Since God tells us that every part of his Word is *"useful for teaching, rebuking, correcting and training in righteousness" (2 Timothy 3:16)*, we have the responsibility to make the connection between what's going on in Sunday school and what's going on in kids' lives.

> **If we don't constantly show kids**
> **how the Bible stories they hear,**
> **the prayers they say and the activities**
> **they participate in are relevant to their lives,**
> **we can't hope to equip them and launch**
> **them on a vibrant walk of faith.**

Our Sunday school program had just begun for fall when the tragedy of September 11th occurred. Not only were we all grieving with the rest of the nation, our church family was reeling with the news that one of our pastors had been on board Flight 11, the first plane to hit the towers. Like teachers in churches everywhere, we talked to the kids, tried our best to answer their questions and led them in making broken hearts to post in the hallways.

Several months after that we were studying Jonah—a reluctant prophet of grace if ever there was one. I had heard from the shepherds that the kids still needed to process the feelings they were having. Would it help, I wondered, if they looked at the story of Nineveh and the events of September 11th through the lens of grace? With that in mind, we used the story to open discussions about the anger that Jonah felt toward his enemies and the idea that they didn't deserve grace. After the first lesson, I got a note from a mom that read, "I don't know what you said, but you pushed open the door for conversation in our house. Thank you."

■ Think about process more than product

It's tempting to envision the kids producing a polished performance in the drama room or creating an elaborate display of creativity in the art workshop. It is in the process of creating, however, that comprehension usually dawns.

I peeked in to watch the Reader's Theater that was taking place in Dramatic Disciples just in time to hear what the fifth graders had learned from the story of Jesus' crucifixion that they had never understood before. "Well, I guess I've never really thought about the fact that the religious leaders and the Romans didn't see Jesus the way we do," said Ashley. "We read the story and we're like, 'Jesus is God's Son; how could you idiots do this?' But they just saw a troublemaker and a loser!"

■ Allow for the Holy Spirit to move and work

It's important to remember that all of us are merely conduits for the Holy Spirit. No matter how many plans or what incredible projects are waiting in the wings, if kids in your class have questions or begin a conversation that signals that doors of the heart have been opened, move out of the way and let the Holy Spirit work.

The Needle that Points True North

When you're frantic to fill a workshop and ready to settle for an activity that has just the teeny-tiniest tie-in to the Bible story, a solid, Bible-based curriculum is the needle of the compass that keeps you pointed toward life change. Anything less is settling for second, third or fourth best. And our time with kids is far too limited to settle for anything but God's very best, week in and week out.

When churches move to multidimensional learning, there's often a great deal of enthusiasm for writing their own curriculum. That's a worthy aspiration, and some churches do a fine job. But there are pitfalls aplenty, and falling into them means giving your kids less than what they need to develop into mature disciples of Christ.

It's always a great treat to visit other churches that are using the multidimensional learning model. I love to see their workshops, check out their structure and listen to what kids are saying as they participate and process. I have visited some churches where kids are totally engaged in authentic learning. They're delving into the workshop activities and into the processing questions that follow. And when they leave, they have a clear idea about how their lives will be different if they live out what they've learned.

I've also seen the opposite happen. It makes me so sad to see kids in beautiful workshop rooms fidgeting distractedly as an adult leader talks on and on. Or doing a craft activity that has to stretch three miles to have any kind of relation to the Bible truth. Or playing a game that's great fun, but that's all. It takes great focus and determination to take your workshops to the next level—the level where kids comprehend, synthesize and apply the Bible truth to their lives.

When you choose or write your own curriculum, these are the hazards you'll want to avoid and the positive goals that will help you provide learning experiences that transform lives.

THE HAZARD	THE GOAL
✦ workshops that are activity driven	✦ workshops that focus squarely on Bible truth
✦ adults talking and doing while children sit disengaged	✦ children are the doers and remain actively engaged
✦ activities that dangle without any way for kids to discover the "now what?" of the Bible	✦ thoughtful processing that ties activities to Bible truth and life change
✦ telling the Bible story in the same way week after week	✦ bringing the Bible story to life in various ways in each workshop
✦ piecemeal presentation of Bible stories	✦ a long-term plan for which stories kids will learn each year
✦ lessons that are structured around only one intelligence	✦ making sure the lessons are experienced through all the intelligences on several levels

What About Making It Fun?

If we're working toward transformed lives, how does fun fit into the equation? In the realm of Christian education, there are usually two extreme opinions about the subject of Sunday school being fun.

One group doesn't understand why kids need anything more than a lecture-based class led by a teacher armed with a Bible and a fill-in-the-blank worksheet. This group insists that kids need "meat" and proclaim that this "talking head" approach was good enough for them, so it must be good enough for every generation.

The opposite end of the spectrum belongs to those hyper-creative folks who try to make every moment of a Sunday school hour resemble a theme-park experience. While this approach may certainly attract kids to Sunday school, there is always a danger that the activities leave little room for any intentional discipleship to occur. This "junk food" approach is just as unbalanced as the "all-meat" diet.

Ideally, an on-target multidimensional learning lesson balances thoughtful and provocative presentation of Scripture with Christ-centered, kid-engaging experiences that open doors of insight and wonder. Inarguably, bringing kids to the place where their hearts and minds are actively seeking to grow in Christ is our primary goal, but fun is a wonderful and essential ingredient when your target audience is kids!

Consider the following two lesson outlines for the story of David. Which do you think would be both kid-engaging and "meaty"?

EXAMPLE ONE

+ The teacher will read the story of David & Goliath from the Bible.

+ The students will then write a script based on the story and practice their scenes with costumes and props.

+ The students will act out the story.

EXAMPLE TWO

+ Students will work in teams to read each scene of the story of David & Goliath and use sound-effects props to decide what they would have heard if they had been present at the battle.

+ As the teacher reads the scenes of the Bible-based story of David & Goliath, each team of students will create the sound effects for their scene as the rest of the class listens with closed eyes.

+ The students will work in teams to record their answers to the following two questions: What are the biggest giants in your lives? What does God want you to use to fight these giants?

Example One: While creating a script for the story and acting it out is challenging and fun, the stimulus is so open-ended that kids could be quite frustrated trying to accomplish this feat in the hour or less that we have on Sunday morning. A concern would also be that the activity is so time-consuming that kids wouldn't have any time for the "so what?" of the lesson.

Example Two: The second example has three benefits. First, the kids actually delve into the Scripture twice in the lesson, once on their own as they prepare their sound effects, and again when they are performing. Secondly, the teams with their eyes closed get a different perspective of the story. We all think about what we would have *seen* that day, but listening for *sounds* brings the story to life in a new way that causes kids who have heard it before to sit up and pay attention.

Finally, experiencing the story in this format gives time for the kids to analyze the information…

> *Why does God want me to know about battling giants?*
> *I haven't seen any lately!*

and synthesize it…

> *Oh yeah, there **are** giants in my life—fear, worry, illness, loneliness, that mean kid at school.*

so they can apply God's "slingshots"—prayer, faith in promises from God's Word, caring friends, parents and teachers—to defeat the giants.

The Fizzle Factor

If you've ever undertaken a home improvement project, you know what it's like to start with great enthusiasm. Then you get tired of the mess, the work, the trips to the home improvement store, the lost weekends. You look at your project in process and ask yourself, "What was I thinking?" You'd almost rather have a root canal than keep at it until you've conquered every last detail.

Oh boy, does the same fizzle factor ever apply to churches who plunge into multidimensional learning! You come away from a conference with your creativity and energy in high gear. This is gonna be great! You get started on the rooms. It's hard work, but the results are ever-so-worth-it. You write some wonderful workshops—kids and volunteers think they've died and gone to heaven. The well of creativity seems bottomless. Wouldn't it be terrific if that first surge of energy lasted forever? Here's a pithy little quote that goes right to the heart of the fizzle factor.

The problem with life is that it's just so daily.

While your workshop rotation program goes on month after month, life simply doesn't let up. The vacuum cleaner burns up, your kids have crises at school, your spouse's job goes away, your parents need your help to move to a retirement center, your transmission goes out and your hard drive crashes. At some point it begins to feel like life pulled the plug on your creativity and it all went down the drain. Or you get sick just like other people do. Unfortunately, I learned this lesson first-hand two years ago.

The month before we kicked off our fourth year of rotation Sunday school, I was diagnosed with stage-two breast cancer. The same week I received the results of my tests, my husband's job was eliminated. To further complicate matters, because of some staffing changes in the children's ministry department, I was writing month-to-month while try-ing to manage all of the other parts of my ministry. It was a hard year, to say the least. As God would have it, that year I was writing the Year of Faith curriculum, so many of the life applications I wrote for kids to process were issues that I was struggling with as well. There were many grace-filled moments and plenty of unexpected gifts amid the rigors of working at a time when I was not at my best, but it's not an experience I'd be anxious for you to share.

Even at the best of times, when you aren't dealing with major or minor life challenges, there are those days when you just don't feel creative, when you can't make anything appear on the blank paper in front of you. I learned long ago that writing is a cooperative dance between the Holy Spirit and me. My friend Charla loves it when she calls to see how the writing is going and I excitedly proclaim "The Holy Spirit is in the house!" But sometimes, for whatever reason, I'm very much alone and the ideas are mediocre.

Those of you in children's ministry leadership positions know just how demanding your job can be. Besides recruiting, buying supplies, setting up your Sunday school environments, supervising the Wednesday night mid-week staff, putting together the Christmas program, coordinating the children's choir, writing for the newsletter, supervising interns, planning, staffing and executing summer camps, you also need to invest some of yourself in your staff. Adding "writing curriculum" to the list is enough to push most of us over the edge. My advice to you is this.

**When you are undone by all that you have to do, listen to Jesus' words to Martha when she was overwhelmed by the choices she had made.
"Martha, Martha" the Lord answered, "you are worried and upset about many things, but only one thing is needed. Mary has chosen what is better, and it will not be taken away from her."**

A Source of Help

Over the years, many of my friends in rotation model churches have found themselves loving the model but drained and discouraged from keeping up with writing and implementing lessons. Knowing how God has blessed the work at our church, some of these friends have asked for my help. Those who used the curriculum I've developed came back with positive reports about enthusiastic staff and changed lives among the kids. Soon I received more and more requests to share.

As I've written curriculum over the years I've given it to God. If it was part of his plan to have it published as a resource for other churches, I trusted Him to make it happen.

It happened! Workshop Zone™ curriculum is now available from Cook Communications Ministries. If the concepts you've read in this chapter resonate in your soul, let me invite you to look into Workshop Zone™. Its evangelical, Bible-based, multi-intelligence lessons have been tested and refined with several "batches" of kids. I'm so happy to be able to offer you what has taken years to create. It's the next best thing to coming to your church to personally help and encourage you.

Expanding the Shepherd's Role

Whether you write your own curriculum or purchase one, let me encourage you to consider enriching the shepherd's role. In our church, shepherds play a key mentoring role with the kids in their groups. They do much more than show up at workshops with an extra pair of willing hands. These dedicated servants make a nine-month commitment to lead one "flock" for the entire school year. Since the children travel to a different workshop each week, shepherds provide a vital continuity and personal connection for the class. They spend the first 20 minutes of each week working on specific spiritual formation activities with their kids. These include building community, helping kids find their "prayer voice," leading disciple-making activities and giving kids a global view of missions.

Here's a sample Sunday morning schedule for shepherds at Christ Church of Oak Brook.

■ 15 minutes prior to the start of Sunday school

A primary aspect of the role of the shepherd is to build community and a sense of a small group on a faith journey together. To facilitate an inviting, kid-welcoming environment, shepherds arrive in the classroom 15 minutes before the beginning of the Sunday morning program. This gathering time provides a way for the shepherds to interact with kids one-on-one as well as allowing the kids to get to know their classmates. Familiar activities such as jacks, card games, pick-up-sticks, Barrel of Monkeys® or Mad Libs® can be kept in a game box in the classroom to provide a comfortable way to break down barriers and keep the kids engaged.

■ Beginning of class time until 20 minutes after the hour: Shepherd Time

During Shepherd Time the shepherds lead the children in activities that help them incorporate spiritual disciplines into their lives. Each Sunday of the month is dedicated to a different exercise.

First Sunday: Spiritual Formation

Spiritual Formation exercises utilize the memory verse for each unit. The children read the Scripture together, then reflect and respond to the Scripture in terms of transformation—how it affects their lives and helps them grow in Christ-likeness—rather than simply information. The questions (and occasional props) allow the children to give voice to their feelings and needs and help to create a sense of community in the group. After processing the verse, students play a game to help them to memorize the scripture.

Second Sunday: Prayer

The class participates in a focused prayer activity. Several prayer models and activities provide a variety of experiences to help kids discover and nurture their own prayer personalities.

Third Sunday: Missions

Just as we spend time teaching kids to reach up to God in worship and reach in their hearts in order to grow, it's also vitally important to teach them to reach out to share the Good News. The mission model that is presented in Workshop Zone is called the "Adopt-a-Missionary" program. To give kids a personal experience of missions and missionaries, every class adopts a missionary family. During the third Sunday of every rotation, the students learn about their missionary family and the country in which they live and serve. Kids compose class emails and letters and pray for their adoptive families. Stewardship of money, time and talents is also a focus of this time as we lead children to embrace all aspects of the Great Commission.

Fourth Sunday: Worship

Every fourth Sunday groups leave their classrooms after attendance is taken and go with their shepherds to a large group worship room. Shepherds sit with children to encourage respectful and joyful worship in community. The children's director or leader can use this time to reinforce the month's rotation theme with a mini-sermon and carefully chosen songs. Suggestions are given to create kid-focused liturgy and structure that help kids better understand the worship fingerprint of "big church."

Fall Kickoff, Fifth Sundays, Advent and Lent

As with any routine, there will be times when the above pattern does not apply. On the first Sunday of the fall kickoff, for example, kids participate in games and activities that help them get to know the other members of their class and their shepherds. During Advent and Lent, activities may focus on the important traditions of the church calendar. One or two months of the year may have a fifth Sunday. This is a wonderful time for an extended worship followed by classroom review, games and fellowship.

If you find the idea of expanding the shepherd's role in your program appealing and you'd like to explore it further, take a peek at this sample shepherd lesson from *Workshop Zone®, The Year of Faith.*

SESSION GOALS

Over the course of the year, we'll explore different prayer models and experiences to help your students find their "prayer voices." The first model we'll explore is A.C.T.S. (Adoration, Confession, Thanksgiving, and Supplication). Today's lesson will focus on Confession.

■ Step One: ACTS Prayer Model

Supplies

____ *a large, colorful poster with "A.C.T.S." on it.*
     Include eye-catching pictures, colors and graphics.
____ *PVC pipe*
____ *wooden dowel*

___ *sheets of paper*
___ *markers*

+ **Who remembers what the letters on this poster stand for?**
+ **Do you need to use fancy words to talk to God? Explain.**
+ **Why talk to God, anyway?**

Last week we talked about Adoration. It's good to start your prayers by praising God and telling him all of the reasons you think He's great.

Today we're going to talk about the second letter, "C" which stands for "Confession."

Confession means recognizing and admitting to God that we have done or said something wrong. Even though God already knows what we've done, it's important to admit it and ask Him to forgive us.

Let's see if I can illustrate for you how important it is to confess our sins when we pray.

■ Step Two: Modeling Confession

Use the PVC pipe as a megaphone. **One thing I really want you to understand is that God is waiting to hear from you. He wants you to talk to him and he wants to answer you. But there's something that can get in the way: SIN!**

Lower the PVC pipe and speak in your natural voice.

✦ **Can you name some of the sins we might need to confess to God?**

Encourage kids to mention things that are likely to be a problem for elementary children. As they come up with suggestions—lying, cheating, using bad language—write each item on a separate sheet of paper. Crumple the papers and have kids stuff them into the PVC pipe.

Speak once again through the PVC pipe full of "sins." (The paper will muffle your voice, but be sure to mumble to make the effect complete.) **The lines of communication with God get clogged up when we have unconfessed sins in our lives.**

Lower the pipe and speak directly to the kids. **So now you understand, right?** They will say, of course, that they couldn't understand you. Hold the PVC pipe up and repeat the phrase once more. **Got it?** After they say "No!" again, repeat the statement without speaking into the pipe.

In other words, sin gets between us and God. He wants the sin out of the way when we come to talk to him. God makes that happen when we specifically tell him our sins and say, "I'm sorry. Please forgive me and help me not to sin."

Use a dowel to push the paper out of the PVC pipe. Hold the pipe up to your mouth and speak through it again.

Confession reopens the lines of communication with God. His Word assures us that "If we confess our sins, he is faithful and just and will forgive us our sins and purify us from all unrighteousness" (1 John 1:9).

■ Step Three: Prayer

Begin with the following prayer. Pause for kids to silently confess their sins, then finish the prayer.

> **Dear Heavenly Father,**
>
> **We praise you and worship you. You are an awesome God, full of power and wisdom. We know we can trust you, and you show your love to us in so many ways. We know we sometimes fall short of pleasing you. Hear us now as we silently confess our sins to you and ask for your forgiveness.** Pause. **Thank you for forgiving us and for forgetting our sins as soon as we confess them to you.**
>
> **In Jesus' name, amen.**

Faith-Hiking with Kids

My family and I love to vacation in Colorado. We spend a lot of time hiking the trails of Rocky Mountain National Park, exploring new trails each time we visit. We learned many years ago how important it is to choose the right hike to begin our trail blazing. Our first hike is always characterized by well-marked, wide paths that gently climb to a reasonable elevation for Midwesterners used to breathing oxygen-rich air. We cruise along at a nice clip, talking, admiring the scenery, loving the feeling of energy we get from striding up a mountain. We get our hiking legs on that first day. It's an important initial step that prepares us for the harder climbs ahead.

The children in our ministries begin their spiritual journeys by getting their discipleship "hiking legs" from the wide, well-marked paths of God's Word. We present stories of God's faithfulness to the men and women willing to take the journey with Him. Those stories help kids acclimate to who God is.

- ✦ *It is in the process of allowing kids to experience the stories of God's faithfulness that they begin to learn to trust Him more deeply because they see Him more clearly.*

- ✦ *It is in God's Word that kids learn about His promises and grace and begin to form a relationship with Him.*

This is what we must keep at the heart of everything we do.

4 The Power of the Story

After months of planning, preparation, room design and writing curriculum, I (Vickie) walked the halls of our children's ministry area, anxiously trying to assess if the day had been a success. As I passed our storytelling room, a bright-eyed second grader named Shelby was excitedly telling her mom all she had heard and experienced that day. "Mom," said Shelby, "I know it's not possible, but I met Mrs. Noah today! And we sewed feed bags for the animals on the ark. Isn't that cool?" Humbly, I sent up a prayer of thanksgiving. It wasn't about what I had done at all; God had captured Shelby's heart because she had participated in His story.

Every one of us has childhood memories of the stories we grew up with. Through the words of fairy tales and fantastic adventures, our minds painted pictures that shaped our imaginations.

Not only did we listen to the stories with delight, we also became the characters as we acted out each episode with childhood abandon, suspending all real-life boundaries. Some, like Aesop's fables, may have even influenced our beliefs and values—and these were just make believe! God's story is *real!* It changes hearts and minds and offers us authentic experiences of mystery and wonder because it brings us into relationship with the Author of the universe. How natural, then, that God chose to introduce Himself through story rather than "specs" or scientific data.

God's story as He has given it to us opens with the words, *"In the beginning, God…"* And throughout the pages that follow God describes Himself to us as the Creator who longs for our companionship. When we were weak and disqualified ourselves from His love, He sent Jesus to make a way to draw us back to Him.

Though we may not even recognize a hunger for a connection with God, we long to be attached—to belong. This is one of the most basic human needs.

God's story expressed in His Word gives us a place in this world. We are His beloved, created in His image, bought with the blood of His Son. Through God's story we teach children that they are unfathomably precious to God. We show them that God knew them before they were born and is closer to them than their next breath. They are written on his hand, sheltered beneath His wings. In giving children God's story, we help the story go on.

This is a love story. Our calling is to share it so sweetly, so winsomely that children will be caught by the wonder of being loved by the One who gave form to the universe. What began "in the beginning" continues to unfold in the lives of those who love and follow Jesus.

Week after week we unwrap God's story so that children can wonder at it, savor it, comprehend it, and finally choose to become a part of it.

Taken to its simplest form, here's what we say to children every week when they come to our ministry.

**"Here is God's story.
Let's experience it together."**

The Art of Language

> *Hear O Israel: The Lord our God, the Lord is one. Love the Lord your God with all your heart, and with all your soul and with all your strength. These commandments that I give you today are to be upon your hearts. Impress them on your children. Talk about them when you sit at home and when you walk along the road, and when you lie down and when you get up. Tie them as symbols on your hands and bind them on your foreheads. Write them on the doorframes of your houses and on your gates.* — *Deuteronomy 6:4-9*

Have you ever had the experience of sharing God's story, only to discover that after all your talking, the kids haven't necessarily learned? "Language" is a vehicle of storytelling. As Christian educators, we need to understand that language is so much more than words. In fact, when we communicate, words are the lesser part of the equation.

Communication is 42% verbal and 58% non-verbal. The implications for teachers are huge. When we're telling kids about God's love letter, the Bible, more than half of what kids understand is *not* conveyed through words but through non-verbal signals such as our tone of voice. In fact, listeners typically base 35% of what they hear on the speaker's tone of voice. That boils down to the amazing fact that 93% of our communication comes through everything *but* our words. Oh, my!

Do You Hear Me?

Is it any wonder that people so frequently misunderstand each other? Think back to an email message that you've received. Without hearing the person's tone of voice, it's easy to misinterpret the message. We've all learned to be careful with those emails. A friend of mine used to write her emails in capital letters. It seemed to me that she was shouting and being pushy. In fact, her vision was failing and she used capital letters so she could read what she had written!

What does this have to do with multidimensional learning? Plenty! When we are communicating the wonderful stories of Scripture, we need to be doing it with more than just sound bytes. Instead, as Deuteronomy 6:4-9 tells us, we need to live out God's Word in our waking, sleeping, coming and going. We need to allow those sacred words to guide our hands, fill our minds with worthwhile thoughts, and demonstrate God's principles in our homes and workplaces.

There's no such thing as "talking" children into God's kingdom. In multidimensional learning, we do our best to identify and maximize all aspects of language and communication so we can reach kids where they are and speak God's story into their lives.

Telling God's story is an art form, because language is an art form. Words are just a small part of the picture. The way in which we express the words is at least as powerful as the words themselves. There is power in storytelling because the storyteller carries us into the realm of imagination through eye contact, body movement, tone of voice, music and hand gestures. The momentum of the story encourages us to wonder about what will happen next.

Jesus himself chose to teach through story rather than through dogma. And what a master storyteller He was! Stories get under our defenses, challenge our perceptions and stretch our understanding. Stories involve us and make us vulnerable. They leave knots that we need to untangle and resolve. When we deliver the sacred stories of Scripture, we need to be deft in using all the storyteller's skills.

An Unforgettable Lesson

Without realizing it, I (Mickie) internalized this concept when I was a young teenager. One afternoon when I arrived home from school, my mother very calmly called to me. "Mickie," she said, "I want to show you something AMAZING!" The word "amazing" rolled off of her tongue with tantalizing sweetness. She used her finger to beckon me to follow her as she tiptoed into the kitchen, slowly and deliberately. I followed… hesitantly and carefully. I was sure I was going to see something really scary or strange. When she got to the kitchen sink, she suddenly stopped. I froze in my tracks. She paused. I waited with baited breath.

"Do you know what happens EVERY DAY right here?" she whispered, pointing to the back splash behind the faucet. My eyes were wide with wonder.

"No. What?" I replied, thinking that perhaps some mysterious animal lurked behind the kitchen wall.

"Dirt collects from the washing of dirty dishes. When you clean the sink, you need to clean back here, too!"

I was never so disappointed in my whole life. I glared at her and she broke into laughter. She "got me." She knew it and so did I. Her body language carried so much of the importance of what she was trying to teach me that, in the end, I remember her every word. To this day I always wash behind the faucets on all my sinks. The lesson was well learned!

Storytelling and Beyond

The LORD said to Moses... "Raise your staff and stretch out your hand over the sea to divide the water... "Then the angel of God, who had been traveling in front of Israel's army, withdrew and went behind them. The pillar of cloud also moved from in front and stood behind them, coming between the armies of Egypt and Israel. Throughout the night the cloud brought darkness to the one side and light to the other side; so neither went near the other all night long.

Then Moses stretched out his hand over the sea, and all that night the LORD drove the sea back with a strong east wind and turned it into dry land. The waters were divided, and the Israelites went through the sea on dry ground, with a wall of water on their right and on their left.

The Egyptians pursued them, and all Pharaoh's horses and chariots and horsemen followed them into the sea. In the

morning watch the LORD looked down from the pillar of fire and cloud at the Egyptians army and threw it into confusion. He made the wheels of their chariots come off so that they had difficulty driving. And the Egyptians said, "Let's get away from the Israelites! The LORD is fighting for them against Egypt!
— *Exodus 14:15-16, 19*

Could the mind of man ever create anything as exciting as the adventures that take place in the pages of God's Word? This one short passage is packed with spectacular "special effects" that were, in fact, not effects but the real thing—an all-too-human hero following the guidance of God Himself, a dramatic chase scene on a path through terrifying walls of water, the defeat of the bad guys with a satisfying flourish. Stephen Spielberg, eat your heart out!

As we use the multidimensional model to reach a generation of kids who live in a world bombarded with stimulation, there's a temptation we need to defeat. It's oh-so-easy to allow the *activities* we devise to help kids experience God's Word to take precedence over the Bible stories themselves. Resist! Dive into the depths of each Bible story with playful abandon. Unveil the sacred stories of God and honor them as the centerpiece of each workshop.

Do You Wonder?

When you approach the stories of Scripture, ask God to stimulate your sense of wonder. What if you were a Pharisee who happened upon the exchange between Jesus and the centurion who begged for his servant to be healed? What if you were the servant? One of the centurion's soldiers? Someone who was attending the sick servant at the moment he was healed?

Consider the perspectives of animals and even inanimate objects that "witnessed" the story. What about a dove who watched the sick servant through a window of the centurion's quarters and followed when the desperate man sought out Jesus? What about the bed on which the servant lay—was it glad to have a break and get aired when the servant got up and back to his work?

What kinds of obstacles lay in the centurion's path? What kind of day was it? What smells and sounds filled the area of the encounter? What did the centurion say when he got back to the house? Was the healed servant waiting for him at the door? When the servant became an old man, how would he relate this story to his grandchild? How did his soup taste to him that night? What sensations did he feel at the very moment he was healed?

Those of us who have spent our lives in God's Word may find that sense of wonder a bit harder to achieve. When we've taught the stories over and over again, it gets hard to see the words on the page. The familiar begins to lose its impact. That's why we need the Holy Spirit. It is the Spirit who inspired those who wrote the Scriptures, and it is the Spirit who inspires our retelling. The sense of wonder can never be a self-generated thing. It's a holy process. Do you hear the call?

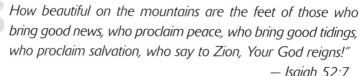

How beautiful on the mountains are the feet of those who bring good news, who proclaim peace, who bring good tidings, who proclaim salvation, who say to Zion, Your God reigns!"

— Isaiah 52:7

Go to the Source

Go to the Scripture *every time* you prepare to tell a story. Even if it's the 562nd time you've taught Noah, read it from the Book. This requires conscious discipline. Acquire various translations and paraphrases so your heart doesn't skid over familiar phrases. Do you speak another language? Read the Bible story in your second language. Try reading the story aloud, giving each character a distinctive voice.

> **Open yourself to God's story**
> **before you presume to teach**
> **it to anyone else.**

Once the sacred story has wrapped its way around your heart, you're ready to make it the centerpiece of your workshops.

This isn't as intimidating as it sounds. Examples of complex and engaging genres of storytelling abound within the pages of Scripture. Exciting narratives, dramatic dialogs, songs of joy, heroic ballads, puzzling parables and tomes of law and history fill God's Book with templates for us to follow and imitate. The possibilities are endless. To prime the pump of your creativity, let's look at five different storytelling methods that will help the kids in your ministry hear God's stories with mind, body and heart.

Notable Narratives

In sophomore English, we learned that a narrative tells a story about an event or experience by answering the "5Ws": who, what, when, where, and why?

The widow of Zarephath's encounter with Elijah in 1 Kings 17 offers a prime example of narrative storytelling. Elijah, following God's directive, has prophesied to evil King Ahab that the wayward nation will suffer a disastrous drought. To keep His prophet safe, God secures him by a stream and sends ravens to feed him. When the stream runs dry, God sends Elijah to receive "bunk and grub" from a most unlikely source—a widow with only one jar of flour and one jar of oil to see her through the upcoming years of famine. It's a wonderful story. We are awed by the miracle of the pots that supernaturally refill with oil and flour, and we cheer when God breathes new life into the widow's only son.

One way to make this tale even more accessible to elementary kids is to use the Bible story as the basis for a first-person narrative from the point of view of one of the characters. When we do this, we help the kids connect with the biblical cast as real people, with real-life lessons to convey. Suppose the widow told the story?

It might begin something like this...

> Do you know what happens when no rain falls on the earth for months—years, even? Plants wilt, crops die. The sun beats down and bakes the ground. Streams and lakes dry up. Soon there is no water. Without water, there is no food. Animals die, and so do some people. Suppose you were in a famine, trying to survive and take care of a small child. Suppose you had only enough food left for one day. What would you say to a stranger who came to your house and asked you to feed him?
>
> That's what happened to me. It is a moment frozen in time for me, like a picture painted on my heart. It was a hot day, as every day for months had been. Each morning I looked up into the scorching sky searching for signs of rain, but none ever came.
>
> The village well was drying up, but the women still gathered there to draw what little water was left and talk about what

was happening in our lives. It was at the well that I first heard the name "Elijah."

I don't know about you, but some of my favorite sermon moments are when my senior pastor "fills in the blanks" around a story that I've heard a million times. A well-written narrative accomplishes the same task for a workshop story. Using commentaries and books from scholars who have researched the political, cultural and social norms of Bible times, we allow kids to get inside a particular moment in time. Through story-telling they learn to know the character and explore his or her world. The widow might stop in the middle of her story to invite the children to help make the daily bread; the kids interact with the story as if they were neighbors who wandered into a cozy kitchen.

When a character responds in ways we would respond or wonders about things that are issues for us, a fleshed-out first-person narrative helps kids discover the spiritual truth for themselves. Suddenly they comprehend why such an ancient message is relevant to their lives.

Skilled storytelling consciously involves several components. A person who "becomes" the character should know the story well enough to tell it from memory. Costumes and props help kids in a storytelling workshop enter a world of imagination where they see the storyteller as a faithful representative of the character. If the volunteer you have recruited for your storytelling workshop is intimidated by the prospect of memorizing a story, however, there are other devices to consider. A journal with pages aged with tea or coffee can be the "recently discovered" archeological treasure that contains the story. An ancient letter from the character to his or her relative (the workshop leader) is another way to get around memorizing the story. However the narrative is delivered, tone of voice, body language, gestures and movements serve to draw the students into the setting.

Interactive Narrative

Yet another narrative experience that leaves memory prints on young minds is the interactive story. I (Vickie) love writing interactive stories. It's an opportunity to use hip, modern language, to play on words and to condense longer stories in order to force the essence of the story into kid-friendly bites. The repetition in interactive stories allows their Creator to write key ideas or phrases on kids' hearts as they "meditate" by listening for their cues to jump or yell or sing or do the wave.

Even more than writing or facilitating interactive narratives, I love watching kids participate in them! When the whole class is being zany, even the most reticent child feels safe to join in the fun. How wonderful to know that when kids think of a wildly joyful, laughter-filled moment, a day at Sunday school might come to mind.

Here's an example of interactive storytelling from *Workshop Zone®, The Year of Faith*. Imagine a dozen excited kids listening intently for each cue, anticipating their responses.

INTERACTIVE STORY SAMPLE

Give these instructions.

✦ *When you hear the word **king**, sound your kazoo like a trumpet announcing a king's entrance. (Doot-doot-ta-doo!) Remember that to play a kazoo, you hum into it. Just blowing doesn't work.*

✦ When you hear **lion's den**, say "deep-deep-down in the dark-dark-den" as you drum on your legs for each word. *(3 slow beats, 2 fast beats, 3 slow beats)*

✦ When you hear the word **pray**, get on your knees, fold your hands in prayer and say the first line of the Lord's prayer: "Our Father in heaven, hallowed be your name."

✦ When you hear the words **hungry lions**, roar and growl and prowl in a circle, looking hungry. When I say "hungry lions" near the end of the story, watch for me to hold up my hand. When my hand goes up, stop your growling and prowling, lie down and say, "Meow!"

✦ When you hear **Daniel**, make a fist, bend your arm at the elbow and pull your fist toward you as you say, "Yo!"

From "Deep, Deep Down in the Dark, Dark Den"
Workshop Zone®, Year of Faith

Long, long ago in the ancient city of Babylon lived a man faithful and true to God. The man's name was **Daniel**. *(Yo!)* **Daniel** *(Yo!)* was 80 years old when he was appointed by the **king** *(kazoos)* to be one of the three main mighty rulers of the land. He was a trustworthy governor in the kingdom. He never lied or cheated or did anything dishonest. Because he was such a good guy and an amazing employee, the **king** *(kazoos)* decided to promote **Daniel** *(Yo!)* to the second-in-command-dude over the whole kingdom.

This decision did not make the other governors very happy. In fact, they were so jealous that they decided to get rid of **Daniel**. *(Yo!)* once and for all. They searched for a way to give him a bad name with the **king** *(kazoos)*, but they couldn't find even one reason to criticize him or his work.

The jealous governors drove themselves crazy trying to hatch a plot against **Daniel**. *(Yo!)* Finally, they realized that if they were going to trap this honest man, their trap would have to have something to do with his faith and dedication to God.

"I know!" said one, clapping his hands in glee. "There is one thing that **Daniel** *(Yo!)* does every day, three times a day, morning, noon and night, no matter what! He **prays**! *(kneel)* We'll talk the **king** *(kazoos)* into making a new law stating that people can only pray to him!" The other governors liked the idea, so they ran to the throne room to set the evil plot in motion.

"O **king** *(kazoos)*, you are the greatest in the land!," the governors said. "We propose a new law to honor you. We think it's a really cool idea for people to **pray** *(kneel)* only to you for 30 days. If anyone **prays** *(kneel)* to any god or man besides you, they should be thrown into the **lions' den** *(deep-deep-down in the dark-dark-den)* to be a midnight snack for the **hungry lions**. *(roar/prowl)*

Darius, the supreme ruler of Babylon, thought this idea sounded pretty good. After all, he was the most powerful man on earth, so why not? "Let's do it!" said the **king**. *(kazoos)* He signed the law and sealed it with his special ring, which meant nothing or no one could change this new decree.

Do you think this new law would change the habit of a faithful man of God? Would fear of the **lions' den** *(deep-deep-down in the dark-dark-den)* be more powerful than faith? Would **Daniel** *(Yo!)* **pray** *(kneel)* in secret to avoid the jaws of the **hungry lions**? *(roar/prowl)* Well…duh!!! **Daniel** *(Yo!)* didn't even argue or complain about this crazy new law. He knew that the most important thing was to please God, not man. He trusted God. He went home, climbed the stairs to his attic, threw open the window that faced the holy city of Jerusalem, got down on his knees and **prayed**! *(kneel)*

Guess who was watching? That's right! The jealous governors! They ran straight to the throne room to tattle to the **king**. *(kazoos)* "The royal law has been broken!" they sang.

Darius was furious. "There will be no mercy!" he cried. "Throw whoever it is into the **lions' den**! *(deep-deep-down in the dark-dark-den)* May his bones be crushed by the jaws of the **hungry lions**!" *(roar/prowl)* "By the way," said the **king**, *(kazoos)* "who broke the law?"

"Well," said the rulers with glee, "it was **Daniel**." *(Yo!)*

This information upset Darius greatly. He liked and respected **Daniel**. *(Yo!)* He tried until sundown to find a loophole to cancel the law, but alas, nothing could be done. Reluctantly he gave the order and **Daniel** *(Yo!)* was thrown into the **lions' den**. *(deep-deep-down in the dark-dark-den)* "May your God, whom you serve continually, rescue you!" said King Darius. *(kazoos)* Then a rock was rolled in front of the door and the royal seal affixed to keep the rock from being moved until morning.

There is no doubt it was dark and scary and stinky down there. The **lions** *(roar/prowl)* were hungry and probably angry at being kept in a dark hole instead of being allowed to roam and hunt in the grasslands.

The Bible doesn't give us any details about the night that **Daniel** *(Yo!)* spent in the **lions' den**. *(deep-deep-down in the dark-dark-den)* But we know what probably happened, don't we? Faced with the greatest challenge of his life, **Daniel** *(Yo!)* **prayed**. *(kneel)*

Meanwhile, the **king** *(kazoos)* returned to his chambers. He didn't eat or sleep. He refused all offers of entertainment for the evening. All he could think about was his trusted advisor in the **lions' den**. *(deep-deep-down in the dark-dark-den)*

When the sun peeked over the great walls of Babylon, the **king** *(kazoos)* hurried to the **lions' den**. *(deep-deep-down in the dark-dark-den)* When it was opened, he called out, "**Daniel**!" *(Yo!)* "Has your God been able to save you?"

"O **king** *(kazoos)* may you live forever. My God has saved me. My God sent an angel to shut the mouths of the **hungry lions**." *(roar/prowl; hold up hand, "Meow!")*

"Fantastic!" said Darius. Then he gave the order for **Daniel** *(Yo!)* to be lifted out of the **lions' den**. *(deep-deep-down in the dark-dark-den)*

Because he had trusted in God, **Daniel** *(Yo!)* didn't have one scratch anywhere on him.

We all have times in our lives when it feels like we're in a **lions' den.** *(deep-deep-down in the dark-dark-den)* When those days of fear and challenge occur, remember to trust God and pray, because you are a child of the *real* **King**. *(kazoos)*

The rhythm of "deep-deep-down in the dark-dark den" will stay with you long after you've read this chapter. It will stay with kids too, and they'll remember to pray, because they're children of the King!

Rally 'Round the Story

Another way to make the story "move" is to post parts of it at various places in your children's ministry area. Teams follow the clues that lead to each part of the story, and kids discover the events and thoughts of the characters "on the road." Then they discuss the reflection questions posted at each station.

When we studied Saul's transforming encounter with Christ on the road to Damascus, kids found parts of Saul's diary on a Damascus Road Rally. Some stations asked the kids to discuss information found in the diary, while others asked the kids to pray or make faith commitments. Each team was formed of smaller groups that discovered information in different ways. The shepherds who accompanied groups on the road rally reported that even kids who were usually shy about participating in discussions were intrigued by the road rally format and felt free to share openly with their peers.

Drama "outside the Box"

When I first started writing drama lessons for our workshops, every one of them looked somewhat the same. Students donned costumes and acted out the story with props, sometimes with written scripts or prompts posted on the walls. All of these devices are wonderful and we still use forms of them in our program. Gradually I learned to step outside my comfort zone and give kids and volunteers a taste of other techniques. I searched for ways to create an environment of discovery, because when kids *discover* a Bible truth, it stays with them in a much more powerful way than if someone simply uses words to "impart" the truth of the story.

Besides the faithful standbys of reader's theater and character interviews, drama can include tableaux, stories told through sound effects, raps and symbolic experiences that creative a "movement memory."

Tableaux

Kids work in teams to create "frozen pictures" of key scenes from the story. Costumes, props and backdrops make staging tableaux fun and involving. Take digital photos of each scene to post outside the drama room or on the church website. After remaining "frozen" for 30 seconds, tableaux can "come to life" with movements and dialogue.

Sound Effects Drama

Visit sound effect websites on the Internet and you'll discover how simple it is to build intruiguing sound props such as a crash box or gravel box. Pick a story that can be enhanced by inviting kids to think about what they might have heard if they had been present when the events took place. There isn't a fifth-grade boy on the planet who can resist an invitation to make noise!

The story of the battle between David and Goliath, for example, works well as a sound effect drama. As a teacher, shepherd or older student narrates, kids can create sounds of an idyllic scene of David as a shepherd. Plastic eggs filled with rice create a gently moving stream; sheep baa; footsteps indicate the coming of the messenger who told David that he was needed at home. Kids love making battle sounds—clanking chains, plastic bats hitting a box, the sickening thud of a rock hitting a water-melon to sound like the stone hitting Goliath's head. Record the story and sound effects on cassette and you have a "radio show" to be used in other ministry settings.

Music and Rap

I find myself turning again and again to Psalms for inspiration when I'm translating stories into different forms. Songs and raps create a sense of fun and whimsy while they appeal to kids who are wired to learn through music. Like interactive storytelling, this sort of story employs the repetition of key words and phrases that get lodged in kids' minds. You know that radio jingle that keeps popping to mind? Bible story raps can have the same effect, but with much more positive content.

Use this form of storytelling even if the musical intelligence isn't one of your preferred ones. Raps "rock" with kids! You can translate parts of the story into easy rhymes set to familiar children's tunes that teams of puppeteers perform. Raps allow teens to be your partners in ministry as they present rockin' rhymes with attitude while kids join in on the chorus with percussion sticks.

SONG EXAMPLE

Joseph had a colored coat.
To his brothers he did gloat
I am father's favorite so
I have this coat you have none…

RAP EXAMPLE

Israel had a new king, his name was Dave
Movin' to Jerusalem, abandonin' the caves!
From this new head man
The palace nanny ran
An' dropped poor Mephibosheth
And watched him land!

Symbolic Storytelling

This storytelling genre is not new—it's actually quite ancient—but we may hesitate to employ it with kids because it involves the interpretation of symbols and metaphors rather than simply swallowing information. What I have discovered, however, is that symbolic storytelling gives kids a kind of "movement memory shorthand" for difficult concepts that works quite effectively.

For example, when we studied the tabernacle, we related each one of the elements within the tabernacle to a different symbolic experience. I wanted the kids to understand that the blood that was shed in the tabernacle merely covered the sins of the people, while the blood that Jesus shed washed them away. To symbolize this "coverage" granted by the brazen altar of sacrifice, then, the kids used a parachute to cover the red scarves used to represent sins. Since we were studying grace, our reflection on this symbol brought out the insight that a parachute can save someone who's falling out of an airplane, just as God's grace saves us from sin.

The oral Tradition and the Great Commission

As wonderful as it is for children to experience Bible stories in a church setting, what we do means little if the truths from these stories fail to carry over into their lives. As the Bible truths begin to speak into kids' lives, we can be confident that God is preparing a new generation of storytellers who will perpetuate the Gospel message in years to come.

Being in the hands of a skilled storyteller is a wonderfully memorable experience. Facial expressions, vocal inflection, gestures, dramatic pauses and exuberant whole body movements give listeners experiences they won't soon forget. Being the teller causes us to remember even more. Being "in character" integrates into our mental responses the motivations and responses of the character we're portraying.

In dramas, kids become the tellers. They step outside of themselves and explore what it meant to be a follower of Jesus in different situations. When they subsequently step back into their own lives, they've been subtly transformed. Another view of discipleship is integrated into their thinking. The power of communication is multiplied because they have been the communicators, not passive recipients.

God's stories have been passed on through oral tradition for many more centuries than they have been in print. Giving kids God's story in rich oral format is one of the most precious gifts we can impart. It's a time-honored tradition that is worthy of resurrecting and preserving for generations to come.

Chewy Questions

God's stories have a power of their own: the Holy Spirit uses them to move the hearts of children. Wise teachers know how to ask questions to facilitate the processing of stories and their integration into kids' lives. Asking great questions is a skill that can never be totally mastered, but it can be carefully honed by years of searching the hearts and minds of children.

It's easy to ask bad questions. They include:

✦ questions that give away the answers.

   "How important is it for us to take time to listen to God each day?" Very important. Duh.

✦ questions with one-word answers that require little or no thought.

   "Do you think Daniel was scared?" Yes. No.

   Refine the question by adding, *"Why did he feel that way? Did it make a difference that Daniel loved and trusted God? Explain."*

✦ questions that are limited to content and ignore application. *"What did Daniel do in the lion's den?"* Prayed.

   Transform this into a question kids can chew on. *"What do you think Daniel's prayer sounded like? If you were in Daniel's place, what would you have prayed?"*

Chewy questions form a tension in kids' minds that's uncomfortable. The question sits there and itches and the only way to scratch the itch is to think about it, process it out loud with feedback from others, and finally settle on an answer that satisfies, at least for the time being. As children express answers, they're building their own ability to communicate their beliefs and their faith questions.

As years pass and social awareness builds, issues will change. Layers of truth will add richness and depth to the story. Those same questions will recur to be chewed on again and again in light of new insights and maturity.

Some folks will tell you that children can't understand and process deep questions until they reach a certain age and stage. But it's been our experience that children's spirituality has little to do with age or brain development. Young children are open to God. Their minds are uncluttered with presuppositions. Sometimes they utter words of wisdom that will knock you flat. So, when you use the art of language to tell God's stories, help children develop their spiritual language by responding to chewy questions. Who knows—you might become the learner when you hear how they respond!

Written Word vs. Spoken Word

A prominent seminary recently did a study of its own mission department to analyze which forms of theological education have been most productive in target ministry areas around the globe. The study confirmed that the people who had accepted the Gospel and were living it effectively were those from "oral" cultures. They were given 60 Bible stories to learn, tell and retell.

This finding gives encouraging support to the practice in multidimensional programs of covering just one story a month rather than blasting kids with 52 stories a year.

Stories learned, explored, plumbed, lived and retold give our kids an incredibly deep Scriptural foundation for their faith journeys. Life change comes from deep understanding and integration into children's lives—not from a barrage of superficial storytelling that moves like a video on fast forward. When we present God's story to our kids, let's plumb the depth. Let them sample the richness of God's Word and gain a love and understanding that grows deeper with every exposure.

Cultures where nationals were taught first to read, translate and study in a literate school setting did not do as well integrating what they said they knew with how they lived. We've mentioned before that people will remember only 20% of what they hear but 70% of what they say. Think of the implications for our children as tomorrow's storytellers!

If we actually remember more of what we say, then we want to be sure that our students are doing a lot of the "saying." This not only gives them the spiritual perspective they need for their life journeys, but also equips them to share the Gospel. We need to consciously give children opportunities to *tell* the stories they hear from us.

Samuel: our Example

Let's look at the biblical example of Samuel—a child whose story we all know so well. Hannah longed for a child. Eli blessed her and she, in response to the gift of pregnancy, gave Samuel back to God for His service.

> *For this boy I prayed and the LORD has given me my petition which I asked of Him. So I have also dedicated him to the LORD. As long as he lives he is dedicated to the LORD.*
> — *1 Samuel 1:27-28a (NASB)*

The rest of verse 28 says *"And he worshiped the Lord there."* Samuel went to be with Eli at the temple, and Samuel worshiped. This is an action word. But it doesn't stop there. Chapter 2 verse 11 says *"...but the boy Samuel ministered to the Lord before Eli the priest."* You see, Samuel didn't just stand around listening to Eli. Samuel was actually *doing ministry.* Scripture mentions it two more times.

+ 2:18: *"Samuel was ministering before the Lord as a boy..."*

+ 3:1: *"Now the boy Samuel was ministering to the LORD before Eli."*

The Word of Lord was rare in those days, and clearly the Lord wasn't speaking to the people through Eli anymore, for even his sons had become a disgrace to him and to Israel. A man of God actually came to Eli and announced that God would have to raise up for Himself a priest—not one of Eli's line. Then in chapter three we have that wonderful story of God calling to Samuel in the middle of the night. Samuel, thinking it's Eli calling, runs to Eli asking him what he wants. It's such a great story, but this is the best part: sometime between the second time God calls and Eli tells Samuel to go back to bed (v. 6), and the third call from God (v. 8), there is a tiny verse of Scripture that should take us by surprise.

> *Now Samuel did not yet know the LORD, nor had the word of the LORD yet been revealed to him. (1 Samuel 3:7).*

What? Samuel didn't know the Lord yet? How can that be? Didn't Scripture tell us at least four times before this that Samuel *"ministered to the Lord"*? How can someone one do ministry and not yet know the Lord? Here is what I (Mickie) believe. Samuel was doing the work of ministry in the tabernacle, working alongside Eli day after day. And Scripture tells us:

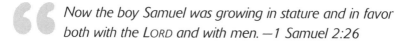

> *Now the boy Samuel was growing in stature and in favor both with the LORD and with men.* —1 Samuel 2:26

In serving the Lord, Samuel was maturing. When Eli understood what was going on after Samuel came to him the third time, Eli said, "It's the Lord calling." Samuel could relate to those words. He may have thought, "Oh, the Lord! You mean the one I've been working for all this time?" When Samuel obediently went to wait for the fourth call he was ready to receive the Word of the Lord. Samuel had been growing up in a "construct" where experiences with God were happening on a daily basis as part of the ministry he was performing. Then when the call came, he had a pre-formed context into which he could place the concept of "the Lord."

In our Western culture, as literate-minded individuals, we place a premium on our children being able to speak certain words before they participate in outward acts of faith. Following the example of Samuel, perhaps we should be putting our children to work in the church, doing ministry. Then when God calls them, they have a context in which to place that call.

If we retain 70% of what we say, 90% of what we say and do and 100% of what we experience, then by all means let's give our kids opportunities to say, do and have experiences of God.

Play Language

For a few years I (Mickie) had the privilege of working with children of divorce as a Play Therapist. By this I mean that I counseled these children, but not with talking. Rather I provided for them a place to play out what they were thinking and feeling. As their therapist/guide, I watched how they played and helped interpret some of what they were acting out in order to give them back a sense of power and control over their seemingly chaotic lives.

> **Children tell us a lot about themselves in the way that they play. Play is a language itself, a language through which children learn the most.**

Playing is experience. Children play dress up, school, store, and other adult-related activities as practice for the future. Children who learn to play well tend to become well-adjusted adults. In the child's world of play they can practice lots of different kinds of things to see what fits them, what they like, what they dislike and how to relate to others. We need to be respectful of that play. We need to allow children to play more so that they can practice life in the safe confines of the playing classroom. Why? Because God speaks to children while they play.

In her book, *Joining Children on Their Spiritual Journey*, Catherine Stonehouse tells the story of a young boy who was playing outside and observing ants. During his play he experienced an "ah-ha!" moment: what if he were nothing more than an ant to a someone greater than himself? No one was out there talking to him about the need to respect nature. No one was teaching him about the cosmos or the concept of the micro and the macro. This young boy was about the business of child-hood: playing. And while he was playing he discovered a deep truth.

As teachers of the faith we need to remember that God is ultimately in charge of revealing Himself through His story.

**One of the best ways for children to
learn something is to actively play.**

We need to provide the places for children to play so that God can make Himself real.

✦ **Play can tell us what children think, feel and believe.**

✦ **Play can tell us of pain, conflict and security.**

✦ **When children are playing they can feel powerful and have a sense of control.**

✦ **Play can help children create, reenact and recreate situations that bring hope for the future.**
   —from *Healing the Children of War*, p. 176

In multidimensional learning, we emphasize learning through experi-ences with God's Story. When we make a time and place for children to play in response to a Bible story, we allow them to be open to hearing God in the languages He's given them. All eight of the intelligences allow a child to play out the stories and tell them over and over again so they become an intrinsic part of the child's very being.

Quiet, Inner Places

Jerome Berryman has developed marvelous resources on the topic of Godly Play™. (See them at *godlyplay.org*.) He teaches that God speaks to children on many levels, beginning in the inner, quiet places of their hearts. Other levels of language surround that inner, quiet place. Our mistake is that we assume that *talking* about theology will hit the inner mark of young hearts. In fact, it's the inner quiet place that needs to inform our theology; all the layers of language play upon each other.

One day a young child was playing outside in a new neighborhood. Having just moved from California to Michigan and from a young family neighborhood to an elderly community, this young boy of four was filled with anticipation, looking to find new friends as he had in California. But Michigan looked different outside than California. The sun wasn't as hot, the sidewalks were old, the trees were really big and there were no other children to be seen.

The small boy picked up an ugly broken branch from a tree and dragged it behind him back into the house. "This stick is lonely," the boy said to his mother. The wise mother knew that the boy was not speaking about the stick; he was making a powerful statement about his own feelings through his play, his body language and his words.

"Let's put the stick right here by the front door so that it will be inside with us while we make some cookies, okay?" said the mom.

"That would be good," said the boy. The mother respected the young boy's "language." Her insightful response helped the child express and move beyond his loneliness.

Are you ready to enhance your educational ministry in a way that is respectful of God's ability to speak to children through play?

**Multidimensional learning
is about building constructs
within which children can have
authentic experiences with God.**

Paul to Timothy told be quick to listen and slow to speak. As Christian educators, let's take that advice to heart and listen to the language of our children in their play, their bodies and their words. Let's provide carefully constructed environments where they can experience God's Story and be able to tell it over and over again.

5 Getting Your Church on Board

You need to become a passionate advocate and strategist.

Creating and sustaining life-changing workshops becomes the work of the body, or it does not "become" at all. Your first and fundamental challenge in moving your children's ministry toward this model is gaining the whole-hearted support of your church leadership. After all, you're going to paint walls. That's such a radical thought that it requires layers of approval. And if you dare to paint a wall, what might you do next!

In addition to your skills in children's ministry, you need to become a passionate advocate and strategist. If that leaves you feeling a bit like Moses did about facing Pharaoh, take heart. We're with you every step of the way.

Your Starting Point: Prayer

You're asking your church to make a big change. You're tampering with a system of teaching that has, despite its flaws, brought forth wonderful Christian leaders. You need open hearts—including your own. So begin by bringing your dream to God on a daily basis. Ask others to join you. Submit to God's timing. Countless experienced leaders of this model will tell you that a well-laid foundation is worth the wait. Pushing for overnight change can bring alienation and hang you out on a skinny limb. God has spent years bringing you to the point where you're ready to introduce the idea. Now allow Him to work in the lives of others.

Don't let your enthusiasm take precedence over God's timing. If you feel that making the change to this model is too much for your plate, you are probably correct. So put it on God's plate. It's always good to remember that this is God's ministry. It's not ultimately up to you.

Start at the Top

Because you've been talking with God about this for some time, you've already started at the top! Now it's time to speak to your senior pastor. As any wise marketing person will tell you, you need to speak in terms of benefits to the church. Focus on the good news you're about to share—news that will make this discussion stand out from all the other issues that are demanding attention. We've mentioned before that many churches who move to multidimensional learning report an increase in attendance of about 20% as well as more regular attendance. Appeal to your pastor based on solid understanding of our goal for the church as a whole.

Selling the Concept

Congregational and leadership buy-in for multidimensional learning is essential. This is not just a VBS program in a box that involves setting up some decorations and doing it all by yourself. It is vital that you educate the entire church—especially the leadership—so that they are behind you and your team 100%. Here are suggestions for launching the concept in your church.

♦ *Always begin with your senior pastor. Explain the benefits of multidimensional learning. Make sure your senior pastor is completely on board before you carry your campaign to other groups.*

♦ *Purchase the video produced by Lord and King Associates, Inc. about Multidimensional Learning. It is only nine minutes in length and shows kids in action in workshop rooms, interviews with pastors and educators and explains the power of this concept for transforming lives. You can order this helpful video at www.lordnking.com.*

♦ *Hold a few intergenerational multidimensional learning experiences as part of a church picnic, Advent Party, Easter Party, or other special gathering when parents and children can be together.*

♦ *Ask to speak at the church's next leadership retreat, meeting or adult class(es) and take them through the Mental Pathways Exercise (chapter one) and add the explanation that's found in the Appendix. This exercise will open adults' eyes to the importance of using all the pathways of learning for Christian education. (You can also order a complete training video that includes this exercise from Lord and King Associates, Inc.)*

✦ *Do a multidimensional rotation experience just for one four-week period to give everyone a taste of it. For example, use the four weeks of Advent as a special time. Then return to traditional teaching in January. Repeat the experience during the seven weeks of Lent and then return to the traditional model. You'll be surprised at how many will begin to say, "Why don't we do it this new way all the time?"*

One church used a "Taste of…" idea as a way of introducing the multidimensional concept to the entire church on Rally Sunday. They had hands-on activities from one particular lesson set up all around the perimeter of the church so that adults and children could experience what the new Sunday school might be like—one story, but many different activities and experiences.

The results? Sold!

A Boost for the Whole Church

Many churches tell us that when they do a thorough job of explaining the theory behind the model and give adults their own experiences with multidimensional learning, the response is, "How soon can we get this started?" Moving to this concept can actually become a mission project within a church's own walls. The multidimensional learning model is much more than a marvelous way to teach children about God. Like the proverbial ripples in a pond, the blessings of renewed enthusiasm move gently outward to encompass the whole of your congregation. Churches in our nationwide network consistently report that moving to the rotation model increased their church attendance by at least 20%!

When Dr. Bob Claus of First Presbyterian Church of Morris, Illinois success-fully moved his church to the rotation model, the enthusiastic comments he heard included, "I've never heard the church sound like this or look like this before. It's really cool!"

Casting the Vision to Leadership Groups

Before you speak to church boards and other leadership groups, you'll want to rough out a strategic plan. Now don't panic, it's not as compli-cated as it may sound. When we say "Strategic Plan" most Christian educators glaze over and bail out. Well, at least I do! But let's think of it in its most simple form. Jan Hubbard, author of *Great Spaces, Learning Places,* and I have worked through the strategic plan that follows with several churches. I am indebted to Jan's "business smarts" for many of the ideas that follow.

Strategic simply means "important or essential in relation to a plan of action." Your plan of action is to enhance your educational ministry with multidimensional learning. As you move forward, choose your language with care.

**Let the gentleness of Christ
be your example.**

There is no reason to give offense to people who have faithfully worked in the traditional Sunday school model. When you speak to people about this new concept, please do not use the words "change" or "fix," as if there is something wrong with the way people have been teaching. This will cause needless hurt and put people on the defensive.

Instead, start by hailing the accomplishments of your church's Christian education program. Explain how you want to "enhance" that success and "improve" upon what is good.

Your Strategic Plan is your plan of action to move from your current program to where you want to be. It's composed of the steps that follow. This yellow brick road breaks down the process of change into chewable chunks. So don't be intimidated by it—it's your friend!

Step by Step

One of the first things to do in preparing a Strategic Plan is to take a look at your church's Mission Statement. While many churches have these, few actually make use of them to shape their ministries. This is a great opportunity to examine that Mission Statement and let it become the dynamic driver it is meant to be.

For example, at University Christian Church in Fort Worth Texas, the Mission Statement mentions wanting to partner with people on their spiritual journey. Taking that idea into the educational ministry gave them just the inspiration they needed: the new Sunday school ministry would be called "Journey Land."

Melding your plan with the church's mission statement is one of those key steps that says, "This is a project that belongs to the whole church—it's not just one person's or committee's wild idea."

Next, create a coordinating Mission Statement for your children's ministry. This may take a meeting or two, but it will become your guiding star in the weeks and months to come.

S.W.O.T

Now it's time to research and write a Situation Analysis and Trend Analysis. (Don't run away. It's simpler than it sounds.) This is your opportunity to step back and take a careful look at your congregation. What situations are you facing? What trends are evident in your church and your community?

Your church has a distinct personality. This list of questions will help you identify what's unique about your congregation.

- ◆ *Who are you?*
- ◆ *What does your community value?*
- ◆ *Where does this community put its time and talents?*
- ◆ *How does this community work? Play? Spend money?*
- ◆ *Are the people who attend here friends or acquaintances?*
- ◆ *Do they desire more connection with each other or not?*
- ◆ *Do the people at this church work during the day or at night?*
- ◆ *Has our church been growing in numbers or dwindling?*
- ◆ *In what age group are the majority of our church members?*
- ◆ *Does this match the general age of the population around you?*
- ◆ *Are you reaching the un-churched or the already churched?*
- ◆ *Who is your target audience for new growth?*
- ◆ *How many kids do you have?*
- ◆ *Have many rooms do you have?*
- ◆ *What is this building really used for anyway?*

Let these questions spark other questions like this. Take a look at what's happening in the world around you.

◆ *Do children in your community all have computers? Then why doesn't the church?*

◆ *Do children and families in your community spend all day Saturday playing games outside? Then why do you do Sunday school inside all the time?*

It's really not all that difficult to check into what your world is like and plan the best way to reach your kids. In fact, it's an essential part of building a dynamic ministry.

While some congregations may get lost in the "paralysis of analysis," an amazing number of church leaders completely ignore these important issues. This is how you capture the trends that help you grow. Look at every trend that affects the children and families in your ministry. Then design a program that meets their specific needs.

Set Goals and objectives

What do you hope to accomplish and when does it need to be done? Make lists of goals and put a target date by each one. Allow for flexibility, but *do* attach dates. An undated project is certain not to get done.

Cast the Vision

You've already brought leadership on board. Now it's time to get the whole congregation pumped about the wonderful things that are in store for the kids in your ministry. Use the ideas listed earlier in the chapter to create multidimensional experiences that will leave everyone hungry for more.

Build Your Teams

You need responsible teams of people who will bring about every aspect of your new program. There's no one set of teams that works perfectly for every church, but here's a good starter list. Consider forming a:

> ✦ *Curriculum Team*
> ✦ *Teacher Team*
> ✦ *Marketing Team*
> ✦ *Room Design Team*
> ✦ *Shopping Team*
> ✦ *Costume Team*

Your Strategic Plan should then develop into a specific Working Plan. At this stage your teams can put together their plan of action on a timeline, make lists of things to do, when they need to have be accomplished and an estimate of what each step will cost.

Marketing

Have one of your teams write a Marketing Plan. This simply means devising a way to let everyone know what you are doing. It's "vision casting" to the congregation. This step gets the adults and children alike excited about what is to come, helps them to buy into it, take ownership, volunteer their time and resources, and encourages everyone to attend.

One church used digital pictures to "market" what was happening in their education space. Each week as the work progressed, they took pictures of the rooms and the people working in them and posted the photos of the work crews around the church. People started to look for the posters. Excitement built. What's that? Who's doing it? Can I help so my picture will be displayed next week? (Essential truth: We're all hams waiting to be photographed!)

Another church put blurbs in the weekly bulletin that read like a continued story. You can be very creative with your marketing strategy. Have fun! You'll find people ready to give both time and resources to the exciting new ministry that's growing within their very walls.

Come and Visit!

There's nothing quite as persuasive as taking a group from your congregation to visit a church that's already doing multidimensional learning. Seeing truly is believing! Consider sending selected leaders to the National Conference in Chicago. They'll come away with renewed enthusiasm and a wealth of new ideas.

Another approach is to invite one of the many experts in this field to come to speak at your church. Or sponsor a regional training event. I'd be thrilled to help you do that. You may contact me directly at *Mickie@ cmamerica.com.*

The video mentioned earlier, *Introduction to Multidimensional Learning,* by Lord and King Associates, Inc. is an excellent tool for getting people inspired. It will let your congregation see kids delving enthusiastically into multidimensional learning activities. They'll hear from excited pastors and educators who give witness to what this model of Christian education has done for their churches. And it clearly explains why this approach to learning is so effective in building young disciples of Christ.

Even Jesus found that people are reluctant to listen to hometown prophets. Visiting another location or bringing in an expert, whether live or on video, can be just the spark you need to get everyone saying, "What a great idea—let's do it! How can I help?"

Sample Strategic Plan

Here's a sample Strategic Plan. Jan Hubbard has contributed greatly to this format; I've added a verbal spin that's unique to the way I approach things. Use this plan as a basis for creating one of your own. It's flexible, so adapt it to work for you!

I. Mission Statement

Write your mission statement, coordinating it with your church mission statement. Make it clear and succinct.

> **Example:** *To implement multidimensional learning in a rotation model in Sunday school classes for grades 1 through 5 at (name of church) beginning (month) of (year). To encourage the children to experience biblical truths and faith stories so they may know and experience God and come to own their faith.*

II. Situation Analysis and Trend Analysis

Your strategic plan needs to include a basic situation and trend analysis similar to the one below.

Issues we face in Christian Education

+ Immature church-goers
+ Inability to find volunteers
+ People expect "someone else" to provide for their children
+ The "entertainment" mentality
+ The "we've always done it this way" mentality

Today's statistics

In our children's first 18 years of life, they spend

+ 15,600 hours in school
+ 15,288 hours in front of the TV/Video
+ 74,232 hours of possible hours at home
+ 832 hours at Sunday school/church

In General

+ Boys like to move.
+ Girls like to talk.
+ Educational expert David Elkind said, "Junior high school boys should not be made to go to school. Instead, someone should take them out and have them build a boat."
+ Men are doers.
+ Women are talkers and listeners.

What is the main teaching style of the church?
TALKING!

Retention is the key to learning. We remember

+ 10% of what we read

- 20% of what we hear
- 30% of what we see
- 50% of what we see and hear
- 70% of what we say
- 90% of what we say and do
- 100% of what we experience

Communication is:
- 42% verbal
- 35% is tone of voice
- 7% is word usage (context)
- 58% non-verbal: body language, physical presence, hand motions
- 35% + 58% = 93%
- 7% is the actual words we speak!

Therefore *we want to present the message of God's Word through all eight of the mental pathways for learning that God gave us.*

One story, many workshops
> *Art Workshop*
> *Cinema Workshop*
> *Drama/Puppetry Workshop*
> *Media Workshop*
> *Music Workshop*
> *Study Workshop*
> *Geography Workshop*
> *Missions Workshop*
> *Faith Issues Workshop*
> *Body Movement Workshop*

Computer Workshop
Storytelling Workshop
Cooking Workshop
Market Workshop
Worship Workshop
Ecology Workshop

Our Goals
- ✦ *Experience the story through many points of entry*
- ✦ *Keep children's interest piqued*
- ✦ *Make use of multiple intelligences*
- ✦ *Teach content–emphasize your theology*
- ✦ *Give children contact with lots of caring adults from within their church community*

Central Scripture
"And these words which I command you this day shall be upon your heart; and you shall teach them diligently to your children, and shall talk of them when you sit in your house and when you walk by the way, and when you lie down, and when you rise." (Deuteronomy 6:6, 7)

Our church's statistics
- ✦ Number of children (list all categories: nursery, preschool, K-6, Jr. High, Sr. High) on rolls: _____
- ✦ Current Attendance
    High Sunday: _____
    Average Sunday: _____
- ✦ Projections for 1 year for these categories: _____

Analysis of Space available for Multidimensional Learning

Permanent dedicated space?
Multiple use space?
Flexible space?

Budget Available ____

Target date for start-up ____

III. Goals and Objectives

Goal 1: To Cast the Vision

Objective 1.1: Transition Consultant and CE Director to meet with CE committee and clergy staff to explain the vision on _____ (date)

Objective 1.2: As many as possible attend Children's Ministries of America Regional Event _____ (date) and National Conference on _____ (date)

Objective 1.3: Provide pulpit supply for congregational understanding of what is being proposed/presented on _____ (date).

Objective 1.4: CE Director writes Strategic Plan with the teams on _____ (date)

Goal 2: To Build the Teams

Objective 2.1: Create a Design Team

> **Task:** *CE Director to call and invite key people to serve as the coordinating Design Team, overseeing the implementation of the new Sunday school model by _____ (date).*

Objective 2.2: Develop a Curriculum Team

> **Task:** *CE Director to assign Curriculum Expert to form a team by _____ (date).*

> **Task:** *Curriculum Expert and team review all available curriculum and make recommendation to Design Team by _____ (date).*

Objective 2.3: Develop a Marketing Team

> **Task:** *CE Director to appoint a Marketing Team Leader to develop the marketing plan ideas by _____ (date). Ideas may include: publicity to the kids, Power Point presentation to adults, brochures, meetings, coffees, bulletin inserts, web page advertisements, fact sheets, etc. to promote the vision of multidimensional learning. Refer to the Situation and Trend Analysis and address all concerns.*

> **Task:** *Marketing Team Leader builds team and begins the following tasks: (List details and dates.)*

As an example, the detail for each task would look like this:

Task: *To develop a Brochure.*
— Action: Mr. Jones will write it by
  _____ (date)
— Action: Committee to meet and approve
  _____ (date)
— Action: The office staff will print, compile and send it by
  _____ (date)

Objective 2.4: Develop a Teacher Team

Task: *CE Director to appoint Teacher Team Leader by*
  _____ (date)

Task: *Teacher Team Leader to Recruit Shepherds and
Workshop Instructors for start date of _____ (date)
(List details of meetings and actions to be taken, along with
dates)*

Objective 2.5: Develop the Building Team

Task: *CE Director to appoint a Building Team Leader by*
  _____ (date)

Task: *Building Team Leader to form Team by _____
(date). (One approach is to have one person heading up
one workshop and building their lists and volunteers for their
workshop.)*

Task: Develop lists of purchases and jobs to be done, assign names of volunteers and dates of actions to be taken by _____ (date)

Goal 3: Select Curriculum and Space

Objective 3.1 CE Director call meeting of Curriculum Team and Building Team for _____ (date) to finalize plans for workshop spaces based on curriculum

Goal 4: Training Sessions for all Teams

Objective 4.1: Marketing Team Training conducted by CE Director and Marketing Team Leader on _____ (date)

Objective 4.2: Train Teachers by _____ (date)

Task: Train teachers on implementing multidimensional learning. This includes:
✦ *Gifts Discovery,*
✦ *Multi-Intelligence Inventory,*
✦ *Hands-on experience with the model, and*
✦ *Off-site visits to existing rotational churches.*

Goal 5: To Implement Physical Design

Objective 5.1: Building Team to take Designer's specifications and distribute to team members for planning of purchases and job assignments on _____ (date)

Objective 5.2: Basic finish changes and structural changes done by _____ (date)

Objective 5.3: Building Team to "take possession" of rooms by _____ (date)

Tasks: Following Designer's specification sheets, install furnishings, finishes and equipment for each workshop (List details and dates)

Goal 6: To Celebrate and Evaluate the Program

Objective 6.1: CE Director to plan celebration event for all teams and church staff one week before opening day_____ (date).

Objective 6.2: CE Director to schedule Follow-Up meeting for week after opening Sunday for all teams. _____ (date).

Task: Send evaluation forms to all involved the week before opening day _____ (date), asking them to take notes and bring to follow-up meeting.

Develop Your Work Plan

With the help of individual team leaders, put all your objectives, tasks, meetings, deadlines and workdays on a master calendar. Then create separate calendars for each team. Check in with all team leaders once a week.

Remember, this plan is a model. Adapt it and make it work for your congregation. Before long, you'll realize that every painstaking step has been more than worth it!

The Essential Ingredient

In all your work on behalf of God's children, prayer is essential to your success. The importance of constant prayer simply can't be overstated. Those of us who have been involved since this model's inception have experienced an extraordinary number of challenges in our churches and our personal lives. Life happens to all of us. But when we're responding to a strong call from God, difficulties intensify.

My colleagues and I come from different walks of life, different denominations, and different faith journeys, yet we have supported and cared for each other through the rigors of this spiritual journey. I remember speaking of this to Jim Guidone, the Minister of Maintenance at Christ Church of Oak Brook. He had been helpful with the National Conference and was curious about my colleagues. Jim is a man of incredible spiritual insight; he asked me how he could pray for the conference and for the movement itself. I listed for him some of the challenges that my colleagues and I had faced as we worked to move this concept forward. Jim looked at me and said, "Well, obviously God is in this movement or Satan wouldn't be working so hard to try to kill it. What a thrill it must be to know you are doing the Lord's work!"

He was right. We do believe that helping churches improve their educational ministry to children is God's work. It is not ours—it never has been. We are simply being used by God. What a privilege!

God has brought together an eclectic group of men and women and combined their ordinary talents to create something extraordinary for His kingdom.

Through multidimensional learning, God is equipping children with life-transforming faith experiences. He is forming them into the young men and women of faith that this world so desperately needs. We have an enemy who will try to make us stumble on this path. But God is able. God has brought us this far and He will continue to provide faithful men and women strength to bring His Word to the world.

A woman at one of our conferences put it this way: "The best thing is that all the different denominations have come together for one purpose—to bring our kids closer to Christ." With that goal in mind and with constant prayer, you can trust God to help you, no matter what challenges you're facing in your life and ministry.

The Director's Role – Make Faith Soup!

working for
Jesus is
like making
refrigerator
soup.

I (Vickie) once told my friend Charla that if I ever wrote a book, it was going to be about the fact that working for Jesus is like making refrigerator soup. He doesn't waste anything! If I get out of his way, he uses every bit of what happens in my life for his kingdom. Since this was too long for a book title, our shorthand for telling each other that God was transforming difficult events in our lives for his good and glory became this simple phrase: "God is making 'Faith Soup.'"

Two years ago, my life was filled with ingredients for faith soup when I walked through the valley during cancer treatments. By God's grace, I "happened" to be writing the Year of Faith unit for our program. I was very attentive to what God wanted to teach me that year, so of course I "kid-sized" each insight and passed them on to the kids in my ministry. God made a rich broth that year, filled with the nourishment of recognizing Jesus' presence in the people who cared for me, and helping the kids in my ministry begin to realize that they could be Jesus to others.

God's Gourmet Ingredients

Along the way, when I have remembered to hold my ministry with an open hand, God has added so many ingredients that my Faith Soup brims with color and texture.

- ✦ My year mentoring a high school senior girl made be "beef up" (sorry) my approach to teaching prayer and devotionals to elementary kids. Katie admitted to me, "I just don't know how to do this." That was my cue to enrich this part of my curriculum so when "my kids" began their journeys through the precarious teenage years, they would be well established in a daily faith walk with their Papa God.

- ✦ A brainstorming session with my friends Nancy and Dawn about how we could expose and involve kids in missions bloomed into the "Adopt-a-Missionary Project." It pairs individual classrooms with missionary families who correspond for a year at a time, learning from each other about God's global heartbeat.

- ✦ A hallway ministry that was born with the intention to reinforce at home what was happening in Sunday workshops morphed into a way to plant seeds in the hearts of my youngest sheep. I learned to listen with great intention to what kids and parents said to me in that brief time.

> **Zach looks forward to talking to
> you every Sunday. He rattles on about
> the things the two of you talk about
> all the way home.**

> **Michelle makes up songs to her
> Bible verse so she can come tell them
> to you after Sunday school.**

> **The take-home sheets are great,
> but Dominic can't do any more
> homework. He would rather just
> hang out with you and help.**

Because I *listened* and didn't insist on doing things my own way, our hallway ministry, "Kid Central," has become *the* gathering spot on Sunday morning.

A Starting Point

Many directors I've counseled over the last five years admit to me that they're in a "ministry rut." The idea of rotational/multidimensional learning excites them, but at the same time it intimidates. They have done Sunday school the same way for so long that they have only a vague idea what it might mean to be a director in this model. Where do you begin?

At His Feet

> *As Jesus and his disciples were on their way, he came to a
> village where a woman named Martha opened her home to
> him. She had a sister called Mary, who sat at the Lord's feet*

listening to what he said. But Martha was distracted by all the preparations that had to be made. She came to him and asked. "Lord, don't you care that my sister has left me to do the work by myself? Tell her to help me!"

"Martha, Martha,' the Lord answered, "you are worried and upset about many things, but only one thing is needed. Mary has chosen what is better, and it will not be taken away from her."

— Luke 10:38-41

Throughout this book, we have stressed to you the importance of prayer. We all *know* that prayer is important, but it takes so much *time*. Beginning a rotation program is labor intensive. When you are anxious about everything that must be *done* and you think everyone is depending on you to do it, every minute counts.

I'm sure you've heard it before, but I'm going to tell you yet again.

You will minister more effectively if you take time to sit at Jesus' feet.

While you are there, connect with Him about other things than the stress you're enduring in your ministry. Remember that prayer is about relationship. Spend time with your Papa. Let Him hold you on His lap. Rest against His shoulder as He refreshes you, renews you and fills you up. That's the key to embarking on any faith journey. If you are doing this for God, and I'm sure you are, involve Him in the process!

To be honest, there are times when I don't sit at Jesus' feet even though I know I should. After a short time of missing my appointments with Jesus, I begin to feel dull and anxious. Lessons get written, calls returned, laundry done, dinner cooked, but nothing has the power I sense when I'm surrendering every morning and asking God to have His way with me.

On the other hand, when I've had a heart-to-heart with God, laughed with Him, listened to Him, I go about my tasks with the confidence that "the Holy Spirit is in the house!" As a result, even when my mind, body and energy are devoted to "doing," my heart resides at His feet, listening to whatever He wants me to pay attention to, watching where He is working so I can join Him, resting when He tells me to rest. The "Martha" in me can display the works of my faith, but the "Mary" in me needs to attend to the Master.

Bridging Vs. Barging

First, let me say that if you are moving from a traditional program to a multidimensional model, one of your first roles is to be a bridge-builder—not a demolition crew. Over and over again I hear anecdotes of hurt feelings and bitterness when a children's team comes in to overhaul the program without considering the faithful servant hearts who Sunday after Sunday have delivered God's Word to the kids in their care.

Though this new and exciting way of learning may make perfect sense to you, it is absolutely vital that you don't begin your program by bashing the "old way" with criticism and disdain. Instead, take time to listen to the Sunday school teachers, craft leaders and parent helpers who have invested their time and talents to help kids grasp the keys to God's kingdom. Solicit their help in the transition, celebrate them, invite them to be a part of your new venture. Many times, those who have worn the many hats it takes to teach in a traditional Sunday school program make perfect candidates for the role of shepherd. They teach because they like to be with kids. Honor that.

If you approach your transition from this perspective, you may find some of your best advocates coming from these very ranks. There will be some, however, who cannot make the philosophical leap required to embrace a multidimensional learning strategy for Christian education. Some will gracefully retire, looking for the next great thing that God has planned for them. Others, unfortunately, will tear down your efforts at every turn. "Why do we need this new model? The old model was good enough for us and our kids, wasn't it?" "It doesn't look like anything is going on to me. It's all fun and games and no substance!"

Believe me, I know how hard it is to hear these comments. It will take time and diligence to convince your detractors. Some will never come around. Here's the good news: you really only have an audience of One.

 Whatever you do, work at it with all your heart, as working for the Lord, not for men…

— Colossians 3:23

from a Shepherd's Heart

One of the shepherds in our program invited me to share her experience with you. As you move toward a rotation program, you might want to share it with others.

 For so many years I was so blessed to be part of a traditional Sunday school

program. I loved being with the kids every Sunday, listening to their sweet voices pray. But for me, it was always a challenge to juggle every part of the lesson. I was always trying to fit so many things into that hour that I didn't get to do what I really liked— be with the kids.

When we began the rotation model at our church, I immediately knew that shepherding was a good fit for me. Now I can focus on the kids and their spiritual growth. I stayed with my kids from first grade through fifth. When they graduated to middle school, I started over with a new class of second graders. I have really loved being able to see my class grow in their walk with the Lord. It's such a gift. An added bonus is that I think I have grown right along with them.

— Beth Stoy,
Christ Church of Oak Brook Shepherd

Make Like a Sponge and Soak

How does the director's role differ between a traditional program and multidimensional/rotation Sunday school? Some things are the same.

- ✦ your desire to be with kids
- ✦ your insight into the way they are wired

✦ *your commitment to passing God's truth to the next generation*
✦ *your need to recruit!*

Other parts of your job will change drastically.

curriculum

In my mind, this is where you start. You must choose and purchase a curriculum or spend some time writing your own before you start. You cannot confidently recruit shepherds and workshop leaders, design environments or promote the model until you have a plan for what will take place on Sunday morning. Can you imagine sending your child to a school where this core ingredient was not already in place?

A word of warning: as tempting and worthy as it may seem for you to write your own material, doing it well is *taxing*. Take it from someone who has done this for five years (and who is still refining lessons from month-to-month). *There are better uses of your time!*

Whatever route you decide to take, the days of handing a curriculum to a volunteer and saying "See you in May, let me know if you need any- thing" are long gone.

Ideally, a director should be intimately familiar with every lesson for every unit before recruiting the volunteers who will teach.

As you review the material, you will get a sense of the best fit for workshop leaders as well as adaptations you need to make to fit your own particular learning space or supplies. It will also equip you to convey the direction of the ministry for the school year, something parents will want to understand.

Hands-on Involvement

When you first begin a rotation program, there are plenty of logistical challenges. Use the following set of questions to brainstorm just some of the things you need to be thinking about.

- *Do you have a mission statement that is both life-giving and practical? What is it?*

- *What are you going to call your program?*

- *Make a brief outline of what workshops you will offer each month.*

- *How will the rooms be decorated and equipped?*

- *What is the best use of your budget dollars?*

- *What will your shepherds actually do in the classroom?*

- *Will you ask shepherds to commit to a nine-month term to provide consistency, or will you allow job-sharing?*

- *What kind of training will you offer to shepherds and workshop leaders?*

✦ *How will you let parents know where kids are to be dropped off and picked up each Sunday?*

✦ *How will you connect what is taking place in Sunday school with the need for parents to disciple their kids?*

✦ *Who will purchase the supplies for your workshops?*

✦ *Who will set up the rooms?*

✦ *Who will clean up the rooms when Sunday school is over?*

✦ *What is your policy for absences? Who will find the subs?*

✦ *How will you connect with your staff?*

While this list is not all-inclusive, it does give you some idea of just how "soaked" you need to be in the details of the program. You may have workshop leaders who buy supplies and set up the rooms, but you will still have to oversee the purchasing decisions. A whole team of people who can think outside the box may help define the mission statement and core values of the program, but it will ultimately be up to the director to be the guiding force. Like Little Jack Horner, a director must, must, must keep his or her finger in every pie!

The "R" Word

The first three years of our rotation program, I job-shared Sunday school responsibilities with another lay leader. I wrote the lessons, purchased supplies, set up the workshops and trained the workshop leaders. Lynn recruited workshop leaders and shepherds, designed activities for the shepherds and took care of many of the budgetary issues.

Most of the time, this arrangement worked. It was when she left that I discovered how valuable it was for me to recruit for the workshops I was designing. Through conversations and brief leading questions, I soon could discern whether or not a volunteer could tolerate "controlled chaos" and lead drama or movement, or if he or she was better suited to games or science.

While none of us relishes recruitment, it is important both for current staffing needs as well as future health of the program that a director develop a real sense of the gifts and talents of the congregation. I'm always exhausted after the initial fall recruitment because I feel like I've given so much of myself away during the many conversations that are essential to the job. As I listen to the problems, challenges and joys of people's life seasons, however, God is giving me a wonderful opportunity to pray with those in need or celebrate a new passage of hope.

While some may not see this investment in others as a time effective use of your day, consider this. It gives you a moment to minister, if only briefly. And if my life is any indication, God will use those ministry moments to make Faith Soup. What seasoning will He add this time?

The Good News

Does this mean that recruiting will be a life-draining, time-consuming millstone that never gets any easier? Breathe. The answer is no.

Though it does take time to establish a rotation program and grow your volunteer staff, it will happen. Workshop leaders with busy lives like the fact that they commit to teaching one month at a time. They love being able to prepare for the lesson the first Sunday, then perfect the lesson each week as they do it three more times. (When I train I explain to men that they get a mulligan each week. They love the idea of that!) Many are disappointed when it's over; they feel like they "just got it down perfectly" when it was time for the next rotation to begin.

When it's time to recruit for fall, I send a letter to past workshop leaders that includes a scope and sequence and a breakdown of which age-levels will be in each workshop by month. This is best done on whimsical paper, injecting humor and grace. One year I even included a hand-written sticky note reminder to post on the fridge!

Many people do, in fact, call me back to "reserve" their workshop and month. I follow up with calls to those who haven't responded, then start looking for new talent in the ranks of parents and other congregation members or those who are "summer only" volunteers who loved their brief stint with the kids.

After your first year of recruiting, it does, in fact, get easier. Word travels and your workshop leaders and shepherds become your best advocates. Two members of my shepherd team are invaluable recruiters for me. They can explain the program because they have intimate knowledge of what takes place and an intuitive sense of who is wired for shepherding.

How 'Bout a Sample?

Have a look at a recruitment letter I used recently. Perhaps it will kick-start some ideas of your own.

What an awesome summer we have had

in the Children's Ministry Department! Kids had many opportunities to grow. Eagles Soccer Camp, Metamorphosis VBS, Rock N' Canoe Adventure Camp, Journeys with Jesus on Sunday morning and Wild and Wacky Wednesday midweek all provided enough fun to keep kids interested and enough challenge to stretch and celebrate their lives in Jesus. God has shown up in so many places and so many ways that I feel like I've been in the "God-Zone" non-stop. I've seen many kids take their first steps on a faith journey and I've seen kids who have taken giant leaps in discipleship. It's been a sacred experience.

While this whirlwind of activity has been somewhat physically depleting, spiritually it has left me renewed and on fire to jump into fall with new enthusiasm. What a privilege it is to work for Jesus!

We have some exciting changes taking place in Children's Ministry this year. First, the Children's Department will soon take up residence in our new offices near the library. This space will be more central to the kids and families of our church. Many of our rooms will be getting a facelift as we refine some of our workshops, including a dedicated science lab called "The Lab" (yes, clever, I know) and a fun room called "Bible GameZone." To celebrate the discipleship journey we are all on, the name of our ministry will also be changing. Sometime this year, Kingdom Kids will become DiscipleZone! From a personal standpoint, I'm pleased to announce that the workshops that the Holy Spirit has used me to write will be published in January by Cook Communications Ministries. It's all very thrilling!

As you may have guessed, this isn't just another "What I Did This Summer" letter. God has designed you with a kid-shaped space that only children's ministry can fill. ☺ Once again, He needs you to use the gifts He has given you to feed His lambs. I hope you'll be back this year to teach. I've included a scope and sequence and a class assignment by month. **Call me now to reserve your workshop. Don't wait or you'll forget...I know how you are. My direct line is xxx-xxx-xxxx.**

The Glamour and the Glitz —or—Sporting the Right Chapeau

Ok. There really isn't any glamour or glitz. If anything, being the director of a multidimensional program is somewhat like being a mom. In the kids' eyes, you are the "principal" with all of the perks (hugs and big smiles) that come with that title. To your volunteer staff, the maintenance crew, your budget manager and the parents of the children in your ministry, however, you wear many hats.

Volunteer Staff

Your volunteer staff looks to you for wisdom and guidance, for the inspiration and content that will help them survive an hour with third graders, and for clarification of matters of procedure and policy. September is a particularly trying time, because even when you've done some of the same things in the past, it all seems new after a brief three-month sabbatical.

Consequently, for your volunteer staff, I suggest you don either a football helmet or an air traffic controller's headset. Once this ministry core is in place, it's up to the director to call the plays and manage all of the blips that show up on radar.

This grace-filled direction begins in the spring when you begin to ask any current Sunday school teachers (or shepherds if you have already begun a rotation program) to join the shepherd team. Once your teams are in place, it's important to meet with everyone prior to the fall kick-off to discuss the nuts and bolts of Sunday morning as well as the details of the ministry. You need to cover things like:

- ✦ where the shepherd supply boxes are stored
- ✦ the purpose of the classroom game box
- ✦ how to handle administrative aspects of class, such as attendance sheets, visitor cards, registration forms, name badges and offering.

This is also the time to share any changes in policy, procedure, vision or purpose for the ministry as a whole.

Ideally, this part of your world represents not only the manpower that allows ministry to happen; it is the community of faith that partners with you in the sacred assignment of planting seeds of transformation in kids' lives.

Since many children's ministry volunteers, especially those that are parents, sacrifice an adult growth opportunity to be with kids, whenever possible make an effort to connect with and nurture your staff. This might be as simple as a phone call to catch up on what's going on in their lives, or a note of encouragement to brighten their day.

On the other hand, a regular time of fellowship and prayer (with food, of course) will strengthen the bonds of your community. It will provide a heart connection and time of Sabbath for the incredible group of people God has put together on this journey. I can hear your complaint all the way over here in Chicago. *"I don't have the time to do what I need to do now, much less find time to intentionally connect with my staff!"* I understand. I sympathize. I can't endorse that attitude however.

When my Executive Pastor of Discipleship, Dr. Greg Ogden, brought a vision of discipleship communities to our church, I couldn't fathom how he expected me to take time out of my busy schedule to "socialize." But I bowed to his wisdom and tried it. It takes effort, it takes planning, sometimes only a handful of people show up, but I humbly ask him now, "What was I thinking?" Can you imagine what kind of New Testament we would be reading today if Jesus gave his disciples tasks but didn't spend any time breaking bread, sharing tears, celebrating life with those men and women that served at his side?

Never underestimate the importance of investing your time and energy into relationships with the people with whom you are doing ministry.

I'd like to share this bit of encouragement I received in an email from a December workshop leader.

Thank you for making sure we all got together for a "group hug" before Christmas. I feel like I've been so busy I haven't breathed. Lifting that cup of sparkling grape juice for our Christmas toast and watching all of the volunteers' kids clinking glasses brought tears to my eyes. I know some people might not have found this brief time anything important, it is a warm feeling I will carry with me during the holidays.

God bless, Lisa

The Maintenance crew

My director of spiritual formation and my missions pastor (in fact, quite a few people!) tell me that I'm a bit compulsive. I like to have things "just so". This means that for the past five years, I've slapped a hardhat on my head and used part of every Saturday to set up my workshop rooms for Sunday—not moving tables and chairs, but putting the supplies, props and environments together.

When we first started our rotation program, this tendency proved very valuable. For one thing, I got to know the maintenance staff very well. We developed a rhythm and respect for each other that enabled us to work together effectively. I also learned the best, most practical ways to make my ideas a reality, and discovered how to adapt supplies or resources when my first attempt was either too time-consuming or impractical.

Do you have to do this all yourself? No. I'm even getting better. I have a team now that helps me on a regular basis. But it's important to be willing to roll your sleeves up and set up your rooms occasionally. When Sunday comes and you know how to troubleshoot problems with the supplies or environment, you'll be glad you did.

Speaking of supplies and environment, one of the aspects of the rotation model that volunteers find so appealing is the fact that everything needed to conduct the lesson is in the room when they arrive. The experiments are set up in the lab, the craft tables are well-stocked in the art workshop, the puppets and props are laid out on the prop table for performing arts. The ingredients for the day's taste treat are enticingly spread out in storytelling, and the supplies to conduct the shepherd's prayer, spiritual formation or missions activity appear each week beside the game box and offering plate in the designated shepherds' area. This attention to preparation allows the shepherd and the workshop leader to focus on the kids and the lessons.

Budget Manager

Those of you who have been in children's ministry for a while know that you have to be creative and flexible when it comes to spending money. While we would like to splurge on a life-sized camel for the hallway, if it takes budget dollars away from any aspect that would allow kids to interact with their community of faith or facilitate discovery of the life-changing love of Christ, we would be wise to reconsider. Every church handles purchasing and reimbursement differently, so a one-size-fits-all solution to acquiring supplies or environmental enhancements isn't going to work. In order to keep things fresh, current *and* affordable, a director needs to slip on the old thinking cap.

Since I design and write my own curriculum, I am constantly borrowing the best ideas from popular culture while carefully avoiding any entanglements that are non-biblical. I keep a notebook in my purse to write down any ideas that come to me as I walk through the grocery store, Home Depot, Barnes and Noble or the toy store. Then I try to figure out a way to cost-effectively transfer those ideas to ministry.

Working with my wonderful ministry assistant, Linda, I also keep my finger on the pulse of our budget by either searching out and procuring the best supplies for each project, or ordering in bulk from a supply, sport or craft catalog. While I would love to delegate the weekly task of shopping for supplies to someone else, it only works for me after the first week of a rotation. When I buy supplies to equip the workshops for the first rotation, I often find that a supply that I have used in the past has been discontinued or that what I had originally planned to use proves too expensive to buy in quantities of one hundred.

This is when my familiarity with the curriculum and my compulsion to shop for the first rotation becomes such a valuable resource. On the spot I can either find an alternative supply or alter my activity to fit what is available. It's time-consuming, but it keeps my stress down to know that everything that I've put in the room will actually function as the curriculum promises.

Vigilant preparation and dashes and compulsiveness cover most situations—but not all. Once at Christmas I was down with a bout of flu and found myself totally unable to get to church. I gave my dear husband one final task to do in order to complete the setup for the December rotation. Since our church has a live nativity the week leading up to Christmas, I share some of my props with the team who staffs the stable. The most important thing they borrow from me is my manger with life-like baby Jesus. Inevitably, every year there is one Sunday that I must tromp out to the stable early on Sunday morning, slide back the door, letting in a blast of cold air on the cozy animals inside, and retrieve "baby Jesus" for the performing arts workshop.

"Get baby Jesus," I told Greg, "and put him in Dramatic Disciples." Content that I could do no more, I snuggled back to sleep. It was only later that I discovered that baby Jesus had ended up in the wrong room. Without dropping the ball, however, the drama teacher had recruited the smallest second grader to play the part of the Savior. He proudly told his mom that he was Jesus. The storyteller who inexplicably found the infant doll in her room, had talked to "the baby" as she rocked Him during her tale, turning her script into an offering of prayer.

Once again, God reminded me that He can change anything into an opportunity. It's nice to know that we don't have to be invincible because our Abba is in charge.

Parents

What hat would the director of a rotation program wear to interface with the parents who share their kids each week? Do you sometimes feel like putting on earmuffs to drown out the demands or criticism? Are you ever tempted to arrogantly wear a policeman's hat to enforce your way, because, after all, aren't you the expert? Though we play different roles at different times, I humbly suggest that you are both a partner in ministry to parents as well as the coach who hopes to equip and empower them to disciple their kids at home. The correct chapeau? A Cubs baseball hat seems appropriate. (Forgive me—I live in Chicago.) It shades your eyes to help you keep your perspective and the large red "C" identifies whose team you are on.

To successfully guide parents to disciple their children, we need to keep three key issues at the forefront.

1. Help parents (and the rest of the congregation) become aware of and adopt God's perspective of the priority of the spiritual development of children.

…watch yourselves closely so that you do not forget the things your eyes have seen or let them slip from your heart as long as you live. Teach them to your children and to their children after them.

This oft-quoted scripture from Deuteronomy 4:9 reveals God's important directive about children to the adults in their lives. I get frustrated at how often the grown-ups in my world look at children's ministry as a support vehicle for the "real stuff" that's going on with adults. As directors, we have a unique opportunity to speak into the lives of families in our congregation. Whatever it takes, however patient we must be, our divine appointment is to gently refocus the lens to help parents see kids through their Abba's eyes.

2. Help parents set the bar as high for their kids' spiritual experiences as they do for kids' educational and athletic endeavors.

I had to comfort a distraught shepherd recently when the closing prayer had been interrupted by a parent picking up her son early so he could make it to a soccer game. What unspoken message does this convey? Sadly, over and over I see parents who make academics and athletics the centerpiece of their kids' lives. Developing a relationship with Jesus is seen as a bonus, something kids can do when and if they have time, or when there isn't anything more important to do. Obviously not all parents subscribe to this view, but what are we doing to reach the ones who do?

3. Make an intentional effort to equip parents with a Biblical worldview and the tools to cultivate spiritual growth at home.

Children's directors are usually specialists. Designing and implementing events and programs for kids is what we do. Unless our job description is stretched to include "family ministry," we rarely consider ministry to parents as part of our venue.

As for giving parents the tools to disciple their own children, we send home a take-home sheet that may or may not be read and discussed. We put articles in the church newsletter that hopefully move the adults who read them to recognize kids' ability to thrive spiritually, but that's about it. What else can we do?

Actually, quite a lot. Invite parents whose kids are in your program to join you for two months. Have someone bring coffee cake and set up a coffee station. Give the parents some time to fellowship at the beginning of the hour. Then teach one of the lessons that the kids are having that morning in Sunday school. Ask the questions that the kids will discuss. Give the adults time to talk around their tables about how this story is relevant to a situation in their lives or the lives of their children. As a group, decide how this information can be used during the teachable moments that come up.

Spend time praying for each other's children. Ask the Holy Spirit to work. Sure, it's another thing on your plate, but the church-home connection is well worth the effort.

The Hardest and Best Lessons

In the previous section, I made the statement that children's directors are usually specialists. It's my opinion that we need to become "generalists." Let me explain. Our main focus is the children in our ministry, but as generalists we move the lens from telephoto to wide angle.

When someone is hurting, we take time to pray with them. Instead of passing on information about a hospitalized child to the visitation pastor, we go see them ourselves, and maybe smuggle in some ice cream. (Indulge me here—I've spent my share of time on hospital food.)

When a family is in crisis, we come together as a community and provide meals, hold hands, dry tears.

Is it hard? You bet.
Is it what Jesus would do?
I believe He would.

As a director, these may be the best lessons you'll ever teach.

7 Build Your Team

> When your team is in place, it really is more a ministry body than a volunteer corp.

As I (Vickie) begin this chapter, I have experienced the toughest recruiting year in recent memory. Even so, with October just around the corner, there are seven strong leaders for the first grade GodPrints team, 24 shepherds are tending their flocks of 2nd through 5th graders, 45 of the 72 workshop spots are filled for the year, and 14 high school students are hanging out with kids as "Sunday Servants."

I believe many factors have contributed to the fact that I've had to work a little harder to build the team this year. The economy has forced more women into full-time positions, and some long-time volunteers have been invited to be part of a mid-size community or are "growing their soul" in a spiritual formation class. A few frankly, are a bit burned out by years of service and just need a time of Sabbath and refreshment.

Whatever the reason, I learned long ago that the fluctuating seasons of people's lives and situations necessitate flexibility and adaptation of recruiting philosophies and practices. Trying to do things exactly the same every year is like a parent trying to discipline a two year old and a teenager in the same way. If you're a parent, you know that what works in one stage of development doesn't necessarily work forever. So it is with recruiting strategies.

There are some techniques, however, that remain constant, and some positions that are unique to the rotation model. When your team is in place, it really is more a ministry body than a volunteer corp.

The Fall Line Up

As you may have discerned by now, transforming your current program to a rotation model involves quite a bit of your energy and creativity. Let me assure you that it's worth it!

This is truly a Christ-centered, kid-loving way to do ministry.

You, the kids, their parents and all of the servants who are part of this adventure will discover the life-giving renewal that God generates through this gift-based ministry to children. So step out in faith, knowing that Christ's directive to "let the children come to me…" could very well end with "no matter how much work it is!"

**Discerning the right fit for your staff
in each role as you help individuals
grow to their God-given potential is
fundamental in creating a functional,
vision-focused servant body.**

The good news is that diversifying the roles that volunteers can play creates many more pathways to service than the role of "Sunday school teacher." That all-encompassing role usually involves just a gifted few or, when we are desperate, a warm body. The mosaic of gifts called upon in this model means that workshop leaders settle in with a lesson that honors their strengths and interests.

✦ *Shepherds connect with kids on a heart level.*

✦ *Members of the congregation who wouldn't dream of getting
up in front of a class contribute by painting, sewing, designing,
providing hospitality, playing the piano, leading worship with
the kids, sharing a passion for missions, or cleaning up after
Sunday school.*

The old adage, "many hands make light work," is not only your battle cry but your song of celebration!

Moses said to Joshua, "Choose some of our men and go out to fight the Amalekites. Tomorrow I will stand on top of the hill with the staff of God in my hands."

So Joshua fought the Amalekites as Moses had ordered, and Moses, Aaron and Hur went to the top of the hill. As long as Moses held up his hands, the Israelites were winning, but whenever he lowered his hands, the Amalekites were winning. When Moses' hands grew tired, they took a stone and put it under him and he sat on it. Aaron and Hur held his hands up—one on one side, one on the other—so that his hands remained steady till sunset. So Joshua overcame the Amalekite army with the sword.   — Exodus 17:9-13

Even Moses needed extra hands, and God provided trusty sidekicks who kept his arms aloft when they grew trembling and weak. There are Joshuas, Aarons and Hurs in your congregation. With wisdom, discernment and the aid of the Holy Spirit, you'll find them.

Shepherds

Our shepherds at Christ Church are an incredible group of people who make heart-to-heart connections to their kids. Listen to what some of them have to share.

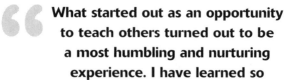

What started out as an opportunity to teach others turned out to be a most humbling and nurturing experience. I have learned so

> much about myself and God from
> the best teachers—our children.

> It has been an incredible experience to
> see the look of excitement and under-
> standing on the children's faces when the
> Bible is brought to life every Sunday.

> Serving as shepherds has been an
> inspiring blessing for my husband
> and me. We've discovered a new and
> exciting world! It's thrilling to see
> God at work with His children!

> The kids ask so many penetrating
> questions. Their questions go to the
> heart of Scripture and our faith. It is a
> blessing to be there to give an answer
> that may plant a seed of faith.

When we began the rotation model at our church, many directors that I spoke with had given the role of shepherd a limited, custodial job description. Our vision for shepherds was quiet different. It addressed kids' need for a consistent and nurturing role model who could connect individual students to each other as a community.

Over the years, what began as a group of dedicated men and women who liked to hang out with kids, pray with them, as well as share some core Bible skills morphed into a richer, more targeted role as the testimonies above clearly demonstrate. The bar we have set for the role of shepherd now reads like this.

The shepherd plays a vital role in our rotation program. These dedicated servants make a nine-month commitment to lead one flock for the entire school year. Since the children travel to a different workshop each week, shepherds provide continuity and personal connection for the class. The shepherd ministry involves building community, helping children find their "prayer voice," conducting disciple-making activities, as well as taking care of the administrative aspects of a Sunday morning program.

Green Pastures

I hope you are beginning to realize that shepherding is the foundation of your rotation program. Cheapening this sacred assignment by recruiting folks with the promise that "all you have to do is take roll and keep the kids in line" means you don't have a balanced approach. Though it's always hard to find people to make a nine-month commitment, there are wonderful parents, singles, grandparents and empty nesters in your congregation who will recognize what a match this role is for their gifts and embrace it as God's anointed commission. In my experience, even those who go into shepherding somewhat uncertainly find it so rewarding that they are soon diving in with enthusiasm. Let's look at a sample Sunday morning schedule as we have outlined it for our volunteers.

♦ A primary aspect of the role of the shepherd is to build community and a sense of a "small group" on a faith journey together. To facilitate an inviting, kid welcoming environment, shepherds arrive in the classroom fifteen minutes before the beginning of the Sunday school hour. This gathering time provides a way for the shepherds to interact with kids one-on-one as well as allows the kids to get to know each other through play. A game box provides familiar activities that initiate comfortable interaction.

Each workshop also has "focus specific" interactive resources that celebrate and stretch different learning modes. So, for example, in the science lab, a video from "Animal Planet" is playing on the television when kids arrive, science books are on the tables, and simple manipulatives are scattered throughout the room for kids to explore. The art workshop has color-by-number posters on the bulletin boards for kids to work on in groups and a Lego center for creative building. The Game Zone's bulletin boards invite a friendly game of Velcro darts or Pin the Tail on Balaam's Donkey.

✦ When class begins on the hour, Shepherd Time begins. During the first twenty minutes of class, the shepherds lead the children in activities that help them incorporate spiritual disciplines as part of our approach of equipping kids with a variety of core concepts. Each Sunday of the month is dedicated to a different exercise.

First Sunday—Spiritual Formation: Spiritual formation exercises utilize the memory verse for each unit with a focus on *transformation*.

Second Sunday—Prayer: Several prayer models and activities offer a variety of experiences to help kids discover and nurture their own prayer personality.

Third Sunday—Missions: Just as we spend time teaching kids to reach up to God in worship and reach in their hearts to grow, we also teach them to reach out to share the Good News. With an emphasis on stewardship of money, time and talent, we lead children to embrace all aspects of the Great Commission.

Fourth Sunday—Worship: Every fourth Sunday the kids leave their classroom with their shepherds and participate in large group worship with kid-focused liturgy that helps them understand the worship fingerprint of "big church."

Fall Kickoff, Fifth Sundays, Advent and Lent: These special seasons and odd Sundays allow for special celebrations around the church calendar, or extended worship followed by review, games and fellowship.

If this approach to shepherding resonates with your spirit, a resource to help you develop it at your own church is at your fingertips. Detailed shepherd lessons form an integral part of the new *Workshop Zone*® rotation curriculum from Cook Communications Ministries.

A Shepherd's Heart

In a sermon at our church last summer, Dr. Ogden outlined the four characteristics of call in a person's life. They're pertinent to our purposes here and worthy of sharing with you!

1. The first characteristic of a call is a focus on a need that you care deeply about. The need may be church-focused or world-focused. It causes you to ask yourself, "Where does the

heart of Christ in me touch the brokenness or need in my world?"

2. Second is a sense of "oughtness." "When I preach the gospel I cannot boast," writes Paul in 1 Corinthians 9: 16, "for I am compelled to preach." In other words, you can recognize a positive burden on your heart.

3. Third is a realization that the mission that accompanies your call to ministry is bigger than you can accomplish in your own strength. With this realization come huge growth opportunities and lessons in surrender.

4. The last characteristic of call is that it comes with a sense of energy and joy!

My experience has been that people who feel called to the shepherd ministry truly do exhibit all four of these characteristics.

+ *They like being with kids and care deeply about them.*

+ *They genuinely have a sense that their mission is to plant seeds in kids' lives.*

+ *They are humble servants who always point to Christ instead of their own gifts or talents.*

+ *They look forward to coming to Sunday school on Sunday morning to hang out with kids!*

From my perspective, these four characteristics form the template for the heart of a shepherd.

Simple Strategy

Now that you have an idea of what a rich shepherd program can look like and you understand the types of people you're looking for, let's get down to the nitty-gritty and talk building strategies.

Begin with the mind-set that the individuals that you recruit as shepherds are on the front lines of ministry. Seek your ideal candidates, knowing that you may not achieve the ideal in the first year or even the second, but somewhere down the road your shepherd team will be full of men and women who are answering their call to ministry.

Next, develop a tool that will guide the conversations you have with volunteers you are considering for this role. For some directors, this might be a very linear tool, like a gift inventory. If that helps you in your discernment process, there are many good inventories on the internet that you can adapt and use to give you a sense of whether the person you are considering has a heart for shepherding.

Personally, I discover the most revealing information from more contemplative questioning. So, my interview document contains the following questions, which I always ask as part of a conversation over a latte at Starbucks.

◆ Tell me about your best experience working with children.

◆ What was your worst experience?

- ◆ Would you describe yourself as a person who is:
    - — An Extrovert or an Introvert?
    - — A Thinker or A Feeler?
    - — A Routine-Seeker or Prefers Variety?
    - — A Control-Freak or Can Tolerate Controlled Chaos?
    - — An Up-front Leader or Behind-the-Scenes Helper?

- ◆ What skills, strengths or talents do you think God has given you? How have you used those for his kingdom?

- ◆ What do you do to stay spiritually healthy?

- ◆ Describe your understanding of what it means to model a Christ-centered life to children.

- ◆ What are the biggest challenges to your trust walk?

- ◆ Where would you like to see God in your journey?

- ◆ Complete this sentence, "I took a risk when I…"

As you can see, there are no right or wrong answers to the questions on this list. But they can help you discover some key factors, such as:

- ◆ *Does this person have any experience working with kids?*

- ◆ *Is he or she fairly mature in faith with a hunger to go deeper?*

+ *Is this person a transparent disciple, easily professing a need to grow?*

It also provides valuable personality information that needs to be considered when putting a shepherd duo together. Two extroverts in the same class might be compatible, two control-freaks will probably not be.

The Finer Points of Bush Beating

Once you have a profile for your shepherd position and a structure to help in your discerning process, it's time to ask God to help you to beat the bushes. If you have a shepherd profile in mind, you will probably already have a list of people you think are shepherd material.

Don't limit your search to parents, though many make excellent shepherds. Engage in conversations with singles and young married couples who don't yet have children of their own. Visit the empty nester's class or ask parents if their children's grandparents might consider the position. Heaven knows that middle school parents won't be allowed to volunteer in their own child's class, so don't let the fact that their kids have moved on stop you from asking them to invest in elementary kids.

If you live in a college community, college kids from your home church are a big hit with the kids. They can often use their service in Sunday school to satisfy required service hours for their college programs. If you are fortunate enough to have a Christian college nearby, call the dean and ask if there are any students who need Practical Christian Ministry hours for graduation. These energetic young people commit to serve every Sunday for a year and often inject a breath of fresh perspective into your program.

**In every conversation you have and as
every new member's profile comes
across your desk, pay attention to the way
the Holy Spirit ignites your instincts.
You're about to discover the wonderful
talent that God plans to use for
His kingdom.**

Your selling points in these conversations should be two-fold.

+ *First, if you design a program that truly allows volunteers to invest in the spiritual formation of kids, your candidates will consider this assignment a call rather than an obligation.*

+ *Second, the activities you design for shepherds should be very user-friendly, with little preparation.*

These statements may seem contradictory; on the one hand I'm telling you that shepherds will play a huge role in discipleship. On the other hand you might think that I'm asking you not to design activities that require too much effort! Though these two points may seem in opposition, they are actually quite congruent.

The rhythm that I introduced in the "Green Pastures" section earlier in this chapter is one way to develop a comfortable routine that frees shepherds to focus on kids when they are leading elements of spiritual formation, prayer, missions or worship. Though the specific activity changes from month to month, the core of the schedule stays the same, fostering a comfortable routine with enough variety to maintain its freshness.

Your interview process needs to take into account not only the answers to the questions on the gift inventory, or the thoughtful disclosures from the discovery questions in your discernment document...

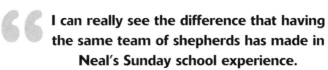

...it's also important to match the personalities of potential shepherds to create a compatible, balanced partnership.

Inevitably, one member of each shepherd team in my program evolves into the nurturer or the fun lover while the other tends to be more oriented towards order and routine. However you designate each shepherd pair, keep in mind that long-term service is your goal. A mom who recently joined our shepherding team told me,

I can really see the difference that having the same team of shepherds has made in Neal's Sunday school experience.

That consistent, caring touch is invaluable. Shepherds are the connecting point. When God leads you to the right people, you're facilitating years of joyful, fruitful service.

Workshop Leaders

In the traditional Sunday school model, we might have posted a recruiting ad that looked something like this.

> **Wanted:** a multi-talented individual with a knack for incredible feats of creativity. Must be able to teach all aspects of a Bible story in one hour, perform mini-dramas, conduct crafts and music, be welcoming and organized, play games, prepare snacks and keep 20 restless kids happy and engaged each Sunday.
>
> **Position Title:** Sunday school teacher.

Whew! Have you ever played this role? I have. I found it exhausting and life-draining… and I am totally addicted to kids! That's why I found the idea of a structure that celebrated my individual teaching style so intriguing.

In a multidimensional model, one person does not have to be a "jack of all trades." Gifted storytellers take students back to Bible times and introduce them to real characters. Those with artistic flair boldly don a smock and paint murals or sculpt with clay or grout mosaics. The drama workshop is led by the uninhibited mother who loves to create teachable moments as kids become the story. It's all much more "doable" and satisfying than the Sunday morning gauntlet that a traditional teacher must navigate.

As a workshop leader in a rotation program, however, individuals have a fabulous outlet for their energy, abilities, gifts and interests. Workshops offer a banquet of choices that include games, storytelling, drama, art, cooking, puppetry, science, music and rhythm, video and life-application.

Instead of teaching a new lesson each week to the same class for all or part of the year, workshop leaders are assigned to one workshop for a month-long rotation. They teach the same lesson to a different class every week for four weeks. Each week workshop leaders refine and perfect their lesson, digging deep into God's Word. I often tell parents that kids who come every Sunday of a rotation are really participating in a complex exegesis of Scripture…only they don't know it, so it's okay.

Imagine being asked to do what you love best with a bunch of enthusiastic kids for four consecutive mornings. There's only one preparation, so you show up…and play! I'm so there, and so are a lot of eager congregation members who wouldn't think of teaching a "normal" Sunday school class. Workshop leaders love their jobs. Just listen!

The term 'life-long learner' brought on new meaning to me when I agreed to volunteer for a month in our Sunday school rotation. Despite the fact that I have been a Christian for nearly 30 years and thought that I had already learned all that I needed to teach a group of 4th and 5th graders, I found myself experiencing many 'ah-ha' moments as I reviewed the curriculum and prepared to teach. I saw God's Word and heard His message

spoken in new, creative and tangible ways through multidimensional learning. What a blessing to have a front row seat to watch the children begin to understand and apply the message to their lives!

My husband and I have been teaching Sunday school for three years. It is amazing to watch as the children discover and live out their faith. The Bible stories are always presented in a new and exciting way. Every time I teach, God shows me something new and I just feel blessed to participate in this program.

We had a phone call recently from one of the members of our church. He and his son were going through the pictorial directory and they came to our picture. The young boy pointed to our picture and said, 'Hey, I know them! They tell us stories!" As teachers in the rotation program, we feel we are building links between generations that God will use to benefit His kingdom.

The rotation format offers the teachers and the students a true freedom to be creative. Children are allowed to grow in their faith because of the openness of the program. The restrictions and walls of a formal lesson have disappeared. I love it!

> "Being a workshop leader has given me the opportunity to explore the life lessons of Christ as they apply to the modern world for today's children. Through the carefully structured and theologically-driven curriculum, I have been able to guide young people into a clear and applicable understanding of God's teachings in an exciting, age-appropriate, hands-on format through music, drama, storytelling, challenging games, and personal reflection. As a teacher, I take away so much from each week's presentation, and I too grow in my spiritual walk through the preparation, presentation, and process of learning with the students and supporting them in their understanding of God's Word."

Wow—I couldn't have said it better myself!

Celebrating Gifts

I described in chapter six that when it's time for fall recruiting, I send home a letter that includes the scope and sequence for the year and the class assignments of each grade level. I have several workshop leaders who jump in to reserve their workshops. One August, after workshop leaders grabbed the opportunity to teach their favorites, I only had a few workshop openings in April and May. And there was a *waiting list* of people interested in teaching workshops that were already taken. That's a pretty good clue that "the Holy Spirit is in the house"!

Let's explore how you put the pieces of the puzzle together to match workshop leaders with workshops. When you unfold a multi-dimensional vision for your congregation, many more people will embrace the chance to serve as workshop leaders than would ever agree to be Sunday school teachers. One reason for this is the grace-filled way that the personalities and strengths of workshop leaders can be celebrated. Once you have decided on a curriculum for your program, the descriptions of your workshops will serve as the "advertisement" to guide workshop leaders to discover the best fit for their gifts, skills and talents.

Here is how we've laid out the workshops in the Workshop Zone® curriculum I'm writing for Cook Communications Ministries.

WORKSHOP ZONE® DESCRIPTIONS

▣ Good Shepherd Inn

Kids settle into a cozy atmosphere and enjoy a Bible storyteller drama, then make and munch a yummy snack that ties in to the story.

▣ Salt and Light Shop

Science and nature exploration leads to wonderful discoveries about our Creator and the stories He gives us to live by.

▣ Mountaintop Productions

The tantalizing smell of popcorn welcomes kids to this workshop where they view and analyze videos that expand the scope of the Bible story.

▣ Faith in Motion

Here's a chance to get rowdy with lively games that challenge kids to recall and relate to important points of the story.

■ Seaside Studio

For the artist in every child! Kids create personal artistic expressions of their spiritual growth and response to the Bible story.

■ Stargazer Theater

Let kids be the stars! This workshop sets the stage for Bible study through all kinds of performing arts—puppets, music and drama.

■ The Temple Court

With a focus on spiritual formation, kids openly explore and express their growing faith with real-life responses.

■ Bible Game Zone

Put those growing minds to the test with an interactive Bible story review followed by fun and fascinating game shows such as Holy Word Squares, Bible Jeopardy, Who Wants to Be a Bible Scholar and more!

Those descriptions will definitely pique the interest of the individuals in your congregation whom God has pinpointed for service!

Once a potential workshop leader has identified a workshop of interest, probing questions further help you determine placement. Many of the same questions you use to interview shepherds can also serve as valuable tools to place workshop leaders. Additional queries should focus on specific experiences and interests in the workshop areas.

So, for example, you might ask someone who has indicated an interest in storytelling whether she would enjoy becoming the character and memorizing the story or would be more comfortable reading the story from the character's diary. You can also ask a potential storyteller to describe the ways he or she would bring the character to life with voice or body language.

Giving examples of specific activities from the curriculum can also shed light on assignments, providing a way for volunteers to become excited about teaching as well as confirming whether or not a particular workshop parallels their gifts.

Perks of the Position

The pleasure that volunteers experience when they teach a creative, gifts-focused workshop takes on an even brighter glow because it involves a manageable, one-month commitment. Congregation members who have a heart to serve will be energized by this thoughtful stewardship of their time and talents. Signing up for one-month stints allows busy people to choose to teach during a month when they expect their schedules to be relatively open. Because of this flexibility and freedom, most people take ownership of at least two workshops during the year.

Another perk that workshop leaders love has to do with the supplies and environment of the workshop. Each Sunday when the workshop leader walks into his or her room, every supply, every prop, every costume, detail or environmental enhancement is in place. Again, this service allows leaders to teach, conduct the activity and really concentrate on what the kids are learning and taking away from the lesson. It may be more work for the administrator on the front end, but it provides consistency in student experience and fosters an appreciation on the part of the workshop leaders. This kind of T.L.C. gives a clear message that they are valued.

Finally, I consistently hear testimonies like those you read earlier. Workshop leaders walk away from this assignment blessed, with a new awareness and sensitivity to God's Word and that "flying high" feeling you get when kids' questions or discoveries have taken you into the "God-zone." Something special happens for adults when they put training wheels on discipleship to help kids learn to worship, grow and serve. It's an experience they cherish, and they'll be back for more.

The Hidden Parts

> **The body is a unit, though it is made up of many parts; and though all its parts are many, they form one body. So it is with Christ. 1 Corinthians 12:12**

For our Body of Christ unit, Dale Olsen, our Environmental Coordinator and artist extraordinaire designed a very cool project for the art workshop. He took ceiling tiles that he bought at Home Depot and cut them into 4 by 4-inch squares. He laid the tiles out as one large, tall rectangle with smaller appendages forming the shape of a cross. On this framework, he used gray paint to draw the outline of Jesus with his hands extended. Then he numbered the tiles on the back so he could reassemble the mosaic.

During the rotation, each child in the art workshop was given a tile and told to draw pictures that represented who they were and what kinds of things they enjoyed doing or felt that they did well. If they received a tile with gray lines on it, the lines were not explained. Some kids drew around the lines; others incorporated them into their work. The lesson focused on who each of us is in the Body of Christ, how God needs all of us to use our gifts, no matter how big or small they are.

We told the kids to watch for the finished picture to appear after the last rotation. When Dale put all of the tiles together, mounted them on a board and hung it in the main hallway of the children's area, it was a lump-in-the-throat moment. Bright, colorful tiles decorated with soccer balls, math equations, dogs and horses and cats, ballet slippers, musical notes and more fleshed out the gray lines to adorn the robe, the arms, the hands and the face of Jesus. Kids stood in front of the display, eagerly finding their tile, standing back to see the whole picture... and they got it!

**It takes all of us and the diversity
of our gifts drawn together in God's love
to form the Body of Christ.**

Remember your battle cry? "Many hands make light work!" What other "hands" can you honor with assignments?

✦ Some churches designate workshop coordinators who purchase supplies, set up the workshop before Sunday morning and troubleshoot for the workshop leader.

✦ An environmental coordinator is invaluable in conceptualizing workshop environments and creating a unified plan for your program theme.

✦ Painters and muralists love lending their talents to transform white walls and drab hallways with bold colors and dramatic Bible scenery.

✦ Those who can sew can contribute by providing robes for the shepherds, costumes for the kids to wear in drama or elaborate wardrobes for workshop leaders to don. Seamstresses are also valuable treasures for the art workshop.

Last year the kids in Seaside Studio made quilt pieces of the Ten Commandments. Jen Irby, a talented mom who sews beautifully, assembled the squares and created a stunning wall hanging for our Bolivian mission project. The kids were so proud that their work would be hanging in the new classroom we had helped to build with our fundraising dollars!

✦ Mission volunteers are priceless resource people who can contact missionaries, design and set up marketing displays and help motivate kids to serve their global family.

✦ Last, but certainly not least, gifted musicians can lend their talents to leading music and worship.

These people are the "hidden parts" who make rich and loving contributions to the Body of Christ. There are talented individuals in your congregation who will eagerly respond to the tap on the shoulder that God delivers through you. The blessings that await them are unimaginable.

Training and Evaluation

8

> ## The right tools make teacher training doable —even enjoyable.

As every Christian Ed Director knows, training volunteers ranks slightly behind recruiting as a task that is difficult to attack with enthusiasm. With new teams of workshop leaders taking over each month, the challenge can be even more daunting. Now ongoing training is truly "ongoing." But take heart. The right tools make teacher training doable—even enjoyable.

Reinventing Teacher Training

First, bite the bullet and realize that if it's at all possible, a face-to-face meeting will be the most productive way to approach training. At a minimum, set up corporate meeting times for shepherds at least three to four times a year:

+ before your fall launch,
+ before Christmas,
+ before Easter and
+ at the end of the year.

These quarterly gatherings will ensure that everyone is on the same page and will provide opportunities for these servants on the front lines of ministry to express both positive and negative feedback as well as to brainstorm and share ideas.

When it comes to training workshop leaders, consider designating one or two Sundays before the new rotation begins as your training date. Workshop leaders can come in after Sunday school to receive their curriculum, be briefed on the mechanics of a typical Sunday morning and hit the highlights of each lesson for the group. It makes your Sunday more hectic, but in my experience, most people prefer this time over evening meetings. Since they are already at church, it's expedient to invest a little extra time for training.

It's All in the Handbook

Be organized! Assemble a handbook for shepherds that includes:

+ the meeting agenda,
+ the first month's curriculum,
+ the rotation schedule and unit overview,
+ samples of parent registration forms,
+ permissions and release forms for students,
+ visitor cards,
+ any application or administrative forms you need from your volunteer, and

✦ a copy of your protection policy.
✦ Information on mission projects, a Sunday morning checklist and a brief synopsis of frequently asked questions might also be helpful.

Teachers will need the curriculum, overview and rotation chart as well as a description of a typical Sunday morning that unpacks the shepherd's role. Include advance warning of any schedule interruptions for the month. It's also helpful to have a handout that explains multiple intelligences and describes the different ways kids learn.

Next, be sure your agenda includes some kind of spiritual food to go along with the snacks and coffee you provide. Share a prayer and a quick devotional that connects to the lesson content or the role these volunteers have elected to play.

Finally, be sure that you don't make the mistake of sitting in a room talking for an hour without giving your volunteers a way to experience their own "ah-ha" moments. Consider the following testimonial about the way University Christian Church in Fort Worth, Texas conducts teacher training.

> *Educator Nita Gilger designs an adult multidimensional learning experience to complement the children's lesson that is coming up. Sunday afternoon, the next round of rotation teachers and shepherds come in to learn about what they will be teaching. Instead of sitting and listening to Nita talk or receiving a packet of material to look over at home, these adults experience the power of the lesson themselves on an their own level.*
>
> *Nita uses film, music, food, drama and games so the adult teachers and shepherds can experience the Bible truth of the*

lesson for themselves. When they in turn teach the children, they can relate their own "ah-ha" moments as the children interact around the components of the lesson.

Though developing these training experiences takes time, the rewards are incredible. Nita has been told many times that her two-hour monthly training sessions are some of the most intense and powerful Bible study these adults have ever had. Imagine what a gift that is for the children—teachers themselves impacted by the lessons they are about to teach.

Sample Training Meeting Agenda

Make your meeting room comfy and wonderful. Go for an instant party atmosphere by having everyone get in on the decorating as they arrive. Set out food, glorious food! Provide name tags.

1. Opening Prayer
2. A little get-to-know you or team-building fun
3. A hands-on devotional—choose a topic and method that ties in to an upcoming rotation
4. Multiple Intelligences Overview
5. Yearly Theme Overview
6. Review job descriptions
7. Typical Sunday Schedule Overview
8. Q & A

Reminders

Keep a "What's On Deck" chart posted in a prominent place. List the workshops and leaders. Set a regular check-in time before a new rotation begins. Whether you choose to do an intense training session like the one described above, or simply a quick touch base, you'll know that your rotation is ready to roll.

Creative Alternatives

Like everything else in the multidimensional learning model, adapt your teacher training to suit the habits and needs of your congregation. Here's a smorgasbord of training ideas and formats to choose from.

+ Provide a take-home kit before each rotation begins. Include the workshop lesson, schedule, news updates and visitor cards.

+ Prior to every unit, schedule a regular workshop leader meeting to go over the curriculum. This gives new leaders an opportunity to hear from those who are more experienced.

+ Have a special shepherd training event. Use a fun 23rd Psalm theme. Go over the shepherd job description from the end of this chapter. Invite experienced shepherds to give their insights. Borrow a shepherd from another church if everyone in your group is new to the rotation model.

+ Try Internet meetings and stay in contact by e-mail. In this age of technology people are often very reachable by this method. Establish an e-mail group or chat room.

+ Post training materials on your church's website. Shepherds and workshop leaders can check in anytime, then email you to let you know that they're up-to-date.

Person to Person

There's no substitute for face-to-face training, fellowship and encouragement, so don't take the easy way out every time. When it seems impossible to get everyone together, set up two alternative times within a couple of days of each other. When necessary grab lunch with a few volunteers at a time. Your volunteers will thrive on the personal attention you give them at these smaller gatherings, and you'll gain valuable insights into how your volunteers and your program are faring.

A Finger on the Pulse

Feedback is a great (if sometimes scary) tool. Consider placing a feedback form in the handbook with each month's rotation.

From the Mouths of Babes

Every now and then it's a great idea to ask for feedback from kids. Get a feel for what they think of their workshop experiences. You'll be amazed at how their responses will help you improve your ministry.

One year I (Mickie) asked a fourth-grade girl to be my assistant. (I've long been convinced that children have the capacity to be leaders in the church, given appropriate responsibilities and mentoring.) When a free sample of curriculum arrived in my office, I asked Shannon to look through it. Her eyes beamed and she went right to the task. She opened the kit meticulously and poured out all the bells and whistles. She sorted through them and then opened the teaching manual. After reading the first lesson, she scooped up toys, put them back into the kit, tucked the teaching manual under her arm and announced, "These toys look pretty silly. I'll just take the book home and write a play about the story. Everyone can take turns with the parts."

And that's exactly what she did. Shannon taught me something very valuable that day. I learned so much from her evaluation that I've never stopped asking the children themselves what they want, need and appreciate.

You'll find a simple evaluation form to use with children in your ministry on p. 210.

CHILD'S EVALUATION SURVEY

1. What's your favorite workshop?

2. What's your least favorite workshop?

3. What's fun for you?

4. Are you making friends in your class?

5. How has being here made your life different?

6. Is there anything you wish we would change?

7. Do you ever invite friends to come with you? Why or why not?

UNIT EVALUATION FORM

Name _____

Workshop _____

What worked well?

What methods or strategies did you develop that we could add to future lessons?

Did you have enough time, not enough, too much? Explain.

Were the supplies provided adequate?

Give some highlights of student responses.

How did you benefit from teaching this month?

Sample Job Descriptions

WORKSHOP LEADERS' JOB DESCRIPTION

Workshop leaders have a wonderful opportunity to offer their energy, abilities and gifts in ministry to children. Eight workshop choices including *(list your workshops)* invite teachers to match their interests and talents to lessons where kids will explore Bible stories and grow in their faith walk. Your commitment is to teach the same workshop to rotating groups of children over a one-month period.

Expectations
- ✦ Professes faith in Christ as Lord and Savior.
- ✦ Has a mature faith.
- ✦ Has a desire to share God's Word with children.
- ✦ Has a talent, skill or spiritual gift associated with the workshop.
- ✦ Will commit your workshop to prayer.
- ✦ Will focus on the learning process rather than perfect products.
- ✦ Will be open to teachable moments and the guidance of the Holy Spirit.

Duties
- ✦ Attend periodic teacher training.
- ✦ Prepare and practice the lesson presentation well in advance.
- ✦ Be on time for class.
- ✦ Report any questions or concerns to *(director's name)*.
- ✦ Notify *(director)* if you will be absent.

SHEPHERD'S JOB DESCRIPTION

Shepherds play a very important role in our Sunday school program. The shepherd is the relationship builder. Shepherds nurture and care for the children in their group. They teach the children for the first portion of class each week. They focus on the children's spiritual formation through Bible verse study, prayer, missions and large-group worship. Although there is no preparation involved in the role of a shepherd, your presence each week is essential to nurture your children's spiritual growth by making them feel warm and welcome.

The Shepherd's Commitment

is from Kick-Off Sunday in September to the End of the Year Celebration in May. Each group/class will have two shepherds. One shepherd per group will be scheduled each Sunday of a rotation.

The Shepherd Is Responsible

for knowing and caring for his/her sheep through:

- ✦ Learning the names of the flock quickly.
- ✦ Moving with the flock through the workshops of each rotation.
- ✦ Encouraging each member of the flock to behave appropriately in the workshops
- ✦ Discovering details about each member of the flock such as:
  - — What school
  - — How many people in the family
  - — Favorite food
  - — Pets
- ✦ Sending birthday, get well, miss you cards
- ✦ Exploring with the children the connections between each workshop within a rotation.

Expectations

+ Professes faith in Christ as Lord and Savior.
+ Loves to be with children.
+ Will pray for the children in your care.
+ Will contact children who are absent or ill.
+ Will commit to staying with the "flock" long enough for the "sheep" to know your voice (9 months).
+ Will be open to teachable moments and the guidance of the Holy Spirit.

Sunday Duties

9:00–9:15: Pick up your Shepherd's box and Shepherd's coat from the Children's Ministry Office.

9:15: Be in the scheduled workshop ready to greet your students as they arrive. Set out the games and puzzles provided so children can be engaged and relating to each other in non-threatening and familiar ways.

Name Badges: Remind each person to wear a name badge. This is important since the workshop leader will not know all of them as you do. Be sure to collect the badges at the end of the workshop and return them to your box.

Attendance: Check off the students' names in the attendance folder as they arrive. Please note when a child has been absent two or more times and send that child a card. The cards are in the Shepherd box and can be put in the Shepherds' Mailbox in the Children's Ministry office. Part of your ministry also includes remembering each child's birthday and sending a card.

Offering: Offering plates will be placed in each classroom. Children can put their offering in the plate or you may choose to pass it during your Shepherd Time. It will be collected and is not your responsibility.

New Children: Please be sure to warmly welcome visitors and complete a visitor's card. Place these in the Shepherds' Mailbox in the CM office. Give visitors a welcome handout to explain the program to their parents.

9:35: Shepherd Time: Begin your Shepherd time with the focus activity that is provided for you each week. These activities are structured using the following schedule:

First Sunday—Spiritual Formation: Spiritual formation exercises utilize the memory verse for each unit with a focus on *transformation*.

Second Sunday—Prayer: Several prayer models and activities offer a variety of experiences to help kids discover and nurture their own prayer personality.

Third Sunday—Missions: Just as we spend time teaching kids to reach up to God in worship and reach in their hearts to grow, we also teach them to reach out to share the Good News. With an emphasis on stewardship of money, time and talent, we lead children to embrace all aspects of the Great Commission.

Fourth Sunday—Worship: Every fourth Sunday the kids leave their classroom with their shepherds and participate in large group worship with kid-focused liturgy that helps them understand the worship fingerprint of "big church."

Fall Kickoff, Fifth Sundays, Advent and Lent: These special seasons and odd Sundays allow for special celebrations around the church calendar, or extended worship followed by review, games and fellowship.

9:45: Turn the class over to the workshop leader. Help the leader with any activities and keep the class in order when necessary.

10:20-10:30: Prayer Activity: Each week you will end the lesson with a simple and fun prayer activity that helps kids learn to express themselves to God. This activity, as well as any supplies needed, will be provided for you. This time is also set aside for prayer requests, joys and concerns.

Dismissal: Establish a ritual to end your class. Say a benediction to close the session, stand at the door and tell each of them good-bye, shake their hands as they go out the door, etc. Be sure to pass out any take home sheets that are in your Shepherd's box.

9 Moses Moments

Are you sure you have the right guy? Please, Lord, send someone else!

The Lord said, "Go, I am sending you to Pharaoh to bring my people the Israelites out of Egypt." But Moses said to God, "Who am I, that I should go to Pharaoh and bring the Israelites out of Egypt?" And God said, "I will be with you." Moses said to God, "Suppose I go to the Israelites and say to them, 'The God of your fathers has sent me to you,' and they ask me, 'What is his name?' Then what shall I tell them?" God said to Moses, "This is what you are to say to the Israelites, 'I AM has sent me to you.'"

— Exodus 3, verses 10, 11, 12a, 13, &14

But what if they won't believe me or listen to me? Lord, you know I'm not very eloquent. In fact, I stutter when I get nervous. Are you sure you have the right guy? Please, Lord, send someone else!

Ah, Moses! Raised in privilege as the adopted heir of Egypt. Trained in battle strategies at the University of the Sun. Indoctrinated in all things Egyptian and worldly. Demoted to humble shepherd in the shadow of Mt. Sinai. Tapped by the God of the Angel Armies to redeem his children from slavery. Is it any wonder that Moses did his best to convince God to change His mind? Haven't you at some time or another in your ministry been gripped by a similar "Moses moment"?

When I (Vickie) first accepted the position at Christ Church to put a rotation/multidimensional learning program into place, I had my share of Moses moments. Though I had been a volunteer in church service for twenty years, I had never been on a church staff. Like Moses, I was a little sheltered in my perspective. As a volunteer, I had been the one to be nurtured and affirmed. Now, I was the one responsible for tending the sheep in my care, both adults and kids. The kids were a breeze; the adults of our congregation were another story. I couldn't believe how many people immediately rejected change of any kind, or dismissed our efforts as unsound and frivolous. My executive pastor, Andy Morgan, served as a filter for many of these criticisms. If he hadn't, I don't know if I would have had the heart to keep going.

Are You Sure, Lord?

The training that had equipped me for this God-breathed assignment was secular. From the time I was in high school, I knew I was going to teach; it was all I ever wanted to do. I received a Bachelor of Arts from the University of Texas at Austin and taught middle school Language Arts and French for eight years before my son Travis was born. For the next eleven years I opted to stay home and raise my kids. I got my kid fix at church and school, volunteering for every position that was offered to me. I knew how to translate knowledge for kids. I had my finger on the pulse of the way they were wired. My faith walk was firm, my Bible knowledge above average, but really, like Moses, I wasn't sure God had chosen the right person for the job.

To further cast doubt on God's choice in my mind, I am part of an incredibly gifted staff. Our pastors have degrees from places like Princeton Theological Seminary, Fuller Theological Seminary and Calvin Theological Seminary. Here I was, an English major from Monahans, Texas, trying to hold my head above water. It was overwhelming to say the least. Not only did I offer up a constant litany to God of why I was unqualified for the position, I began to ask him to release me from my call. Another fine Moses quality.

Like Moses, I stayed the course. It wasn't because of any miraculous storehouse of knowledge that suddenly lodged itself in my brain and helped me to feel equipped. It wasn't that the pace got easier and I felt like I knew what I was doing at every moment. It wasn't even that the pieces started falling into place that first year to confirm that we were on the right path.

I put one foot in front of another and stepped out in faith because, like Moses, I had been called. I had been chosen for a holy assignment to deliver the message of redemption to God's children. Though I was uncertain of everything else, of that I was sure.

Faith-Hiking

We know that Moses persevered in his assignment in spite of his misgivings and feelings of inadequacy. Because he finally gave in and made himself available, God used all of his knowledge of Egyptian culture, his training at "Sun U" and his forty years tending cranky sheep in the desert to produce the most spectacular escape you could ever imagine. When Moses left Egypt with the children of Israel in tow and began his forty-year hike through the desert, God made Faith Soup with Moses' gifts, training and challenges. God can do the same for you.

Getting Your Hiking Legs

The first thing to realize is that hiking with God means you are often going to be stretched beyond your comfort zone. This stretching was what made Moses try to get out of his assignment. It's what made me feel so inadequate when I came as a lay leader into a staff full of the spectacular men and women who pastor our church. If you are an ordained children's pastor you may not know this feeling. But those of you who are in lay leadership positions will completely understand. What I began to humbly admit, however, is that since God doesn't make mistakes, I must in fact have the stuff He could use for this job.

This flexibility test began in August, when our dean of education informed us that the curriculum we had purchased was not consistent with our theology. As I scrambled to begin first rewriting, and then writing from scratch, I realized that I was going to have to let go of any precon-ceived ideas of how this journey would progress. Around December of that year I began to step out in faith because I knew I was hiking an unknown path, advancing with the eyes of my heart even when the footholds weren't evident or easy.

Rather than looking at this time of challenge as unbearable, however, I urge you to recognize God's gentle stretching as a training discipline for the sacred hike you are undertaking.

Training Disciplines

■ The Discipline of Prayer

Once again, never think you are too busy for prayer. An intentional, regular prayer time is your lifeline to God's power. Yet, sadly, when we get overwhelmed by all we have to do, it's often the first thing to go. Several times during my ministry journey I have felt as if my prayer life became stagnant.

The worst episode occurred one week before my eighth, and last, chemo treatment. Weak and depleted, I ended up in the hospital with a pulmonary embolism in my right lung. I felt in many ways that I was in a spiritual desert. The seven previous months had taught me many valuable lessons, but when I prayed during my four days in the hospital, I felt as if I could see my words bounce around the room and hit the ceiling. When I complained to my spiritual mentor, Adele Calhoun, our pastor of spiritual formation, she gave me some simple but invaluable advice about prayer that I would like to pass on to you. Many times, when we are in a difficult season of our prayer lives and everything we do or say seems flat, God gives us the unique gift of His silence. When this happens, we have two choices. We can either quit praying because it seems as if we are alone and abandoned, or we can feed our hunger to be close to Him again and try whatever it takes to get there.

■ Silence

Anxious to reconnect with my Papa and feel the consolation of His presence, I discovered that my prayer life had been in a bit of a rut. Without meaning to, I had put my devotional time in a nice neat box that I could check off of my list every morning when it was accomplished. The first few weeks after I got home, I was so weak that I just sat on my front porch in silence. As I watched the sun filter through the leaves and listened to the birds building their nest in the eaves, Bible verses would come to my mind unbidden. I would repeat them out loud. The longer I sat, the more aware I became of God's presence. Then it occurred to me—I had been filling up my prayers with so many words that God couldn't get a word in edgewise! It was a helpful epiphany. Many times now, my entire prayer hour will be spent in perfect silence, sitting with God and entering that quiet place that allows Him to point out things to my waiting spirit.

■ Lectio

Lectio Divina was another powerful discipline that put some muscle in my prayer life. Many good resources exist that unpack this ancient practice, but in brief, it means to meditate on scripture and let God's Word guide your prayers. A good place to begin practicing Lectio is with the Psalms. Pick a short chapter and read it slowly out loud several times. Savor the phrases and let them hang in the air. Listen to your spirit as you read. What word or phrase jumps out at you?

Now spend some time chewing on that word or phrase or verse. What does it mean to you? Why is it important? What do you sense God is trying to say to you? Talk to Him about the verse and all the ways you see it intersecting with your life and circumstances. Lectio is a simple but potent way to reenergize your prayer life.

■ Take a Walk

Prayer walks take you out of your normal element and plunge you into nature. In effect, you can be in your own private bubble as you carry on a conversation with God. Who cares if the neighbors think you're crazy?

When I prayer walk, I usually follow the A.C.T.S. model of prayer. I begin with *adoration*, telling God all of the reasons I can think of to praise Him for who He is. Then I *confess* to Him all of my sins. I make sure I'm very specific about asking Him to reveal to me anything that I've missed. When I get to "T" I *thank* God for every big and little blessing He brings into my life. *Supplication* is divided into two parts: petition for specific prayer needs for my family, friends and me, and intercession for whoever God puts on my heart.

Because I feel I need constant physical, mental and spiritual refreshment, I always pray for renewal in all of these areas. On my way home, I repeat whatever Bible verse I have been committing to memory and talk to God about my day. And I always, always take a small notebook with me to write down whatever insights God sends my way. Come to think about it, I probably do look a little bizarre during these strolling tête-à-têtes.

■ Binding Prayer

My family calls me the sticky note queen. I post the little yellow billboards everywhere to remind me not to forget to pick up the laundry or take my daughter to the orthodontist or call my sister. I have a similar fetish regarding prayer. Because I want to remember to pray for someone if I have promised to do so, I came up with a way to jog my memory that I've used a lot over the past two years.

As the three of us were working on this book, our lives have seemed to be in constant turmoil. Mickie moved her parents into assisted living, got married, sold her house, and bought a new house. I had some reactions to the medications I was taking, pulled my back out, and had to retrieve information from my hard drive when our server at church crashed. Lois has battled fatigue and muscle pain from fibromyalgia, prepared her heart for her only daughter's move out of state and worked into the night to edit everything we sent to her. During the last stage of the book, when our deadline was near, Lois' ninety-three-year-old mother suffered a stroke.

In all the times we had held each other up in prayer, this time I wanted to make sure that I was faithful. So I picked a favorite bracelet out of my jewelry box, one that sparkles like Lois does, and I bound it around my wrist as the Israelites did their phylacteries. Then every hour on the hour, I offered up a breath prayer for Lois and her mother. "Lord," I said, "this day, hold Lois and her mother to your breast so they can both hear your heartbeat."

No time to pray? Remember Moses? God's staff was ever with him, reminding him not to trust in his own power. And except for the occasional story of Israel's antics, most of Exodus is a record of his conversations with God.

Growing Your Soul

■ Worship

We have three services at our church on Sunday morning and two on Sunday evening. Because our rotation Sunday school is held during the second service and I am often putting the finishing touches on setup or meeting with my staff, I rarely make it to any of the three morning services. Sunday night is our Celebration Service, with contemporary music and an easy family atmosphere. When I can go, that's my service. I don't feel like I have to be "on" like I do in the morning and besides, I can wear my blue jeans!

Oftentimes, however, I'm so tired that I don't make it to Celebration. When this happens too many times in a row, I begin to feel parched, in need of a drink of living water. When we first started the program, this inability to attend worship made me a little bitter. Then I realized that not going to worship was my own fault and no one could do anything about it but me.

Again, adjusting your expectations and rhythm to fit a new paradigm of spiritual practices takes discipline and planning. Though you might prefer one service over another, the most important thing is that you go when you can. It's not about you anyway; it's about worshiping God, who's worthy of worship and hopes to see you there.

■ Community of Fellow Believers

There are times when, like Moses, our hike through life gets so challenging that our faith wavers and begins to fray at the edges. It is at these times that the company of fellow hikers provides the fellowship we need to encourage us.

Our great cloud of witnesses includes the heroes of the faith who earned that title in spite of their shortcomings and failures because they fixed their eyes on Jesus and ran with perseverance the race marked out for them.

In our own lives we need faith boosters, people who encourage us with wisdom and love when circumstances create Moses moments that threaten to defeat us. For me, these faith boosters have been the Ya Yas, my four closest friends in the world. We meet once a week for Bible study, for fellowship, for prayer. We break bread together and share those things in our lives that are "in the vault"—things that we don't tell anyone else. The Ya Yas help me to grow my soul. Had they not been there, I would have wandered in a spiritual wilderness, finding nothing but the next tumbleweed.

If you aren't part of a small group or Bible study, make it a priority to find a group of Christian friends who can help you make it through your Moses moments.

■ Celebrate the Journey

What? You can't figure out why this is a discipline to help you grow your soul? Let's see if any of the following scenarios sound familiar. One of your kids has a soccer game or wants to go to an afternoon movie. You have so much to do to make sure Sunday runs smoothly. You are torn, but after all, you are in ministry. You work instead. Or you are dead tired and crabby because volunteers didn't show up and you had to run yourself ragged during Sunday school. It's a beautiful fall day, but instead of sitting outside to enjoy the day, you catch up on the laundry or go to the grocery store.

All of us get caught up in the obligations and "have tos" of our daily lives. If we don't stop to celebrate the journey, however, the storms in our lives will not only threaten to overwhelm us, they will obscure everything *except* the wind and the rain. From the beginning, God established a rhythm for our days—work followed by rest.

Catch the rhythm. Spend frivolous hours with your kids at the park. Have lunch with a friend even when you don't have the time. Take a walk…take a nap! We all need Sabbath; it refreshes us and renews us. It restores us and fills us with light, so that when we must next be warriors, we are prepared.

■ Practicing the Presence

I was raised in the desert where sand, mesquite and an endless horizon made it easy to lose perspective. It's the same with Moses moments. During those times when God doesn't quite show up as you had hoped, you need to look back the way you came and celebrate the evidence of God's presence in your life.

The Israelites were reminded to *"remember that you were slaves in Egypt and that the Lord your God brought you out of there with a mighty hand and an outstretched arm." (Deut. 5:15) "I will remember the deeds of the Lord...,"* cried Asaph in Psalm 77 during a time of deep distress. And Jesus, knowing that the faith of his disciples was about to be tested to the utmost by upcoming events, instituted a ritual of broken bread and wine and told His disciples to *"do this in remembrance of me." (Luke 22:19).*

The horizon of our perspective becomes clearer when we remember all that God has done for us. In her book, *The God Hunt*, author Karen Mains talks about how she taught her children to hunt for God in their everyday lives. When they experienced an answer to prayer, unexpected evidence of God's care, help doing God's work in the world or unusual timing or circumstances, her kids told her they had experienced a "God Sighting."

We all need to be so sensitive to God's work in our lives that we mentally, emotionally or physically record the God Sightings in our lives. As we reflect on God's faithfulness and provision during our hikes through difficult terrain, we begin to acquire a fresh vision of who God is. We remember other times when the trail was difficult, but we were blessed to have God to lean upon, to blaze our path, placing our feet in the footprints He left in the sand. When we remember, our trust grows…and we bend down to slip on the shoes that He gave us.

Of course, the shoes are too big for us because we still have lots of room to grow. But it's good they are too big because they force us to take one step at a time, and they prevent us from running ahead.

Like the children that we are, we take God's hand and hike on in faith.

Appendix

Multiple Intelligences Survey

PART I

Complete each section by placing a "1" next to each statement you feel accurately describes you. If you do not identify with a statement, leave the space provided blank. Then total the column in each section

Section 1

_____ I enjoy categorizing things by common traits
_____ Ecological issues are important to me
_____ Hiking and camping are enjoyable activities
_____ I enjoy working on a garden
_____ I believe preserving our National Parks is important
_____ Putting things in hierarchies makes sense to me
_____ Animals are important in my life
_____ My home has a recycling system in place
_____ I enjoy studying biology, botany and/or zoology
_____ I spend a great deal of time outdoors

_____ TOTAL for Section 1

Section 2

_____ I easily pick up on patterns
_____ I focus in on noise and sounds
_____ Moving to a beat is easy for me
_____ I've always been interested in playing an instrument
_____ The cadence of poetry intrigues me
_____ I remember things by putting them in a rhyme
_____ Concentration is difficult while listening to a radio or television
_____ I enjoy many kinds of music
_____ Musicals are more interesting than dramatic plays
_____ Remembering song lyrics is easy for me

_____ *TOTAL for Section 2*

Section 3

_____ I keep my things neat and orderly
_____ Step-by-step directions are a big help
_____ Solving problems comes easily to me
_____ I get easily frustrated with disorganized people
_____ I can complete calculations quickly in my head
_____ Puzzles requiring reasoning are fun
_____ I can't begin an assignment until all my questions are answered
_____ Structure helps me be successful
_____ I find working on a computer spreadsheet or database rewarding
_____ Things have to make sense to me or I am dissatisfied

_____ *TOTAL for Section 3*

Section 4

_____ I learn best interacting with others
_____ The more the merrier
_____ Study groups are very productive for me
_____ I enjoy chat rooms
_____ Participating in politics is important
_____ Television and radio talk shows are enjoyable
_____ I am a team player
_____ I dislike working alone
_____ Clubs and extracurricular activities are fun
_____ I pay attention to social issues and causes

_____ *TOTAL for Section 4*

Section 5

_____ I enjoy making things with my hands
_____ Sitting still for long periods of time is difficult for me
_____ I enjoy outdoor games and sports
_____ I value non-verbal communication such as sign language
_____ A fit body is important for a fit mind
_____ Arts and crafts are enjoyable pastimes
_____ Expression through dance is beautiful
_____ I like working with tools
_____ I live an active lifestyle
_____ I learn by doing

_____ *TOTAL for Section 5*

Section 6

_____ I enjoy reading all kinds of materials

_____ Taking notes helps me remember and understand

_____ I faithfully contact friends through letters and/or e-mail

_____ It is easy for me to explain my ideas to others

_____ I keep a journal

_____ Word puzzles like crosswords and jumbles are fun

_____ I write for pleasure

_____ I enjoy playing with words like puns, anagrams and spoonerisms

_____ Foreign languages interest me

_____ Debates and public speaking are activities in which I like to participate

_____ *TOTAL for Section 6*

Section 7

_____ I am keenly aware of my moral beliefs

_____ I learn best when I have an emotional attachment to the subject

_____ Fairness is important to me

_____ My attitude effects how I learn

_____ Social justice issues concern me

_____ Working alone can be just as productive as working in a group

_____ I need to know why I should do something
before I agree to do it

_____ When I believe in something I will give 100% effort to it

_____ I like to be involved in causes that help others

_____ I am willing to protest or sign a petition to right a wrong

_____ *TOTAL for Section 7*

Section 8

_____ I can imagine ideas in my mind

_____ Rearranging a room is fun for me

_____ I enjoy creating art using varied media

_____ I remember well using graphic organizers

_____ Performance art can be very gratifying

_____ Spreadsheets are great for making charts,
graphs and tables

_____ Three dimensional puzzles bring me much
enjoyment

_____ Music videos are very stimulating

_____ I can recall things in mental pictures

_____ I am good at reading maps and blueprints

_____ *TOTAL for Section 8*

PART II

Now carry forward your total from each section and multiply by 10 below:

Section	Total Forward	Intelligence Indicated
1		
2		
3		
4		
5		
6		
7		
8		

Remember:

+ Everyone has all the intelligences!

+ You can strengthen an intelligence!

+ This inventory is meant as a snapshot in time– it can change!

+ M.I. is meant to empower, not label people!

KEY TO THE MULTIPLE INTELLIGENCES SURVEY

Section 1 – This reflects your Naturalist strength

Section 2 – This suggests your Musical strength

Section 3 – This indicates your Logical strength

Section 4 – This shows your Interpersonal strength

Section 5 – This tells your Kinesthetic strength

Section 6 – This indicates your Verbal strength

Section 7 – This reflects your Intrapersonal strength

Section 8 – This suggests your Visual strength

✦ How has God made you?

✦ The person who shares your office?

✦ Your family members and closest friends?

✦ What insights have you gleaned from this exercise about teaching children?

McKenzie, Walter. (1999) Multiple Intelligences Inventory.
Found online at http://surfaquarium.com/MI/inventory.html

Mental Pathways Pie Training Activity

Make a copy of "The Shape of Your Mental Pathways Pie" (p. 29) for each participant. Beforehand, scan the room and divide it into eight sections by tacking up eight sticky notes labeled A-H.

Give these directions.

Look at this list of activities lettered A-H. Rank these eight activities using the numbers one through eight with one being that which is your easiest and favorite thing to do and eight being the thing you wish you never had to do.

Each sentence should be ranked with a different number. We don't want three ones and five eights. Don't think too deeply about it—just give it a go.

Allow two minutes to complete the activity. Then explain that you have divided the room into eight sections labeled A through H. Point out the different sections. Have participants go stand by the letter that corresponds to the letter that they attributed as number one.

Once everyone is beside a letter, point out the sections that have few or no people. Explain that each of these letters corresponds very simply to Howard Gardner's Multiple Intelligences Theory.

Letter A—The Naturalistic Intelligence or Nature Smart

Letter B—The Musical Intelligence or Music Smart

Letter C—The Mathematical/Logical Intelligence or Math Smart

Letter D—The Interpersonal Intelligence or People Smart

Letter E—The Bodily/Kinesthetic Intelligence or Body Smart

Letter F—The Verbal/Linguistic Intelligence or Word Smart

Letter G—The Intrapersonal Intelligence or Self Smart

Letter H—The Visual/Spatial Intelligence or Picture Smart

Explain that the intelligences represent the different ways in which we grab hold of information. Emphasize that we all have all eight intelligences—it's just that some pieces of our mental abilities pie are larger than others. You can use the people themselves as living examples of how these different intelligences work. For example, there may be several people in the Musical Intelligence area, yet you know that they don't all sing in the choir. This just means that the Musical Intelligence is a big part of their lives; it isn't directly correlated to musical talent or ability. We need to use music in our teaching in a variety of ways to help develop this intelligence in all the children.

Next have everyone move to the letter that they designated as their number two choice. Make sure to note that there are completely different clusters now. Explain again the strengths of these different areas. You will know your people, so have fun with this.

Next, tell them to go and stand at the letter they gave the number eight ranking—their least favorite. You're likely to have several people near letter C, Mathematical Intelligence. Have a good laugh with this one, talking about budget problems and balancing checkbooks. Or, say to the people who are now standing by letter A that we should be careful not to ask them to be responsible for plant care at the church

I usually mention that those who are standing by letter D probably dislike like activities like this because they really would rather not do group work. We need to be respectful of them as well.

Now that everyone has had a chance to physically experience their own preferences for learning, they can understand how children learn and how ineffective the sit-down model of education is for them.

Recommended Reading from Vickie Bare

✦ ***When Children Pray,*** Cheri Fuller, Multnomah Publishers, Inc. (Helps parents and Christian educators to establish a mind-set of prayer for kids. Beautifully written with anecdotes that bring the text to life.)

✦ ***Parent's Guide to the Spiritual Growth of Children,*** John Trent, Rick Osborne and Kurt Bruner, Focus on the Family (A basic guidebook for the spiritual stages of children).

✦ ***Multiple Intelligences: The Complete MI Book,*** Kagan Cooperative Learning. (Easy to read and understand explanations of the eight major intelligences originally identified by Gardner as well as sample lessons that can be adapted to a spiritual setting)

✦ ***Growing Up Prayerful,*** NavPress (A great resource from the publishers of *Pray*! magazine that gives creative ways to lay the foundation of prayer in kids' lives. Has a great section of idea books and websites to explore)

✦ ***Teaching Your Child How to Pray,*** Rick Osborne, Moody Press (More ideas to help parents and educators give children a prayer voice. Includes questions for reflection and discussion as well as prayer activities.)

✦ ***Children Demand a Verdict,*** Josh McDowell, Tyndale House (Great apologetics with training wheels!)

Multidimensional Learning Bibliography

Lord and King Associates, Inc.
Mickie O'Donnell Gutierrez

Thomas Armstrong, Association of Supervision for Curriculum Development (www.ascd.org)
  ✦ *Multiple Intelligences in the Classroom*
  ✦ *In Their Own Way*

John Barell, ASCD, 2003
  ✦ *Developing More Curious Minds*

Jerome Berryman, Augsburg, 1991
  ✦ *Godly Play: An Imaginative Approach to Religious Education*

Marcia Bunge, Editor, Eerdmans Publishing Co. 2001
  ✦ *The Child in Christian Thought*

Bruce Campbell, et al, / Paperback, Published 1996
  ✦ *Teaching & Learning Through Multiple Intelligences*

Sophia Cavalleti, Catechesis of the Good Shepherd Publications
  ✦ *The Religious Potential of the Child*

Carolyn Chapman, Lynn Freeman, Paperback, Published 1997
+ *Multiple Intelligences Centers and Projects*

Richard Coleman, CSS Publishing, Inc. Lima, Ohio, 2002
+ *Gospel Telling, The Art and Theology of Children's Sermons.*

Robert Coles, Houghton Mifflin Company, 1990
+ *The Spiritual Life of Children*

Howard E. Gardner, Basic Books
+ *Frames of Mind : The Theory of Multiple Intelligences/Tenth Anniversary Edition*
+ *Multiple Intelligences : The Theory in Practice*
+ *The Disciplined Mind*
+ *Intelligence Reframed : Multiple Intelligences for the 21st Century,*

Vigen Guroian, Oxford University Press, 1998
+ *Tending the Heart of Virtue: How Classic Stories Awaken a Child's Moral Imagination*

Carla Hannaford, Great Oceans Publications 1995
+ *Smart Moves, Why Learning Is Not All in Your Head*

Eric Jensen, ASCD, 1998, 2000, 2001, 2002
+ *Teaching With the Brain in Mind*
+ *Arts With the Brain in Mind*
+ *Learning with the Body in Mind*
+ *Different Brains, Different Learners*

Spencer Kagan, Miguel Kagan, can be reached through
www.KaganCoop.com
- ✦ *Multiple Intelligences : Evaluating the Theory*
- ✦ *The Complete MI Book*

David Lazear
- ✦ *Seven Pathways of Learning : Teaching Students and Parents About Multiple Intelligences*
- ✦ *Seven Ways of Knowing : Teaching for Multiple Intelligences*
- ✦ *Seven Ways of Teaching : The Artistry of Teaching for Multiple Intelligences*

Marlene LeFever, Cook Communications, 2002
- ✦ *Learning Styles*
- ✦ *Creative Teaching Methods*

Vivian Gussin Paley, Harvard University Press, 1999
- ✦ *The Kindness of Children*

David Sousa, Corwin Press, Inc. 2001
- ✦ *How the Brain Learns (2nd Edition)*

Nancy Spence and Jane Connell, Abingdon Press 1998
- ✦ *From BC to PC: A Guide for Using Computers*

John Walsh, Moody Press, 2003
- ✦ *The Art of Storytelling*

Phyllis Wezeman, Anna Liechty, Kregel Publications, 1996
- ✦ *Hymn Stories for Children*

Video Resources by Lord and King Associates

✦ Play: The Transformational Language of the Child
✦ Multidimensional Learning 101
✦ Multidimensional Learning–What's it all about? (short)
✦ Virtual Tour of Chicago area Churches

Joshua: Courageous Faith

Workshop

Faith in Motion

Grades 4-5

◆ **Scripture Source**

Joshua 1-6

Trusting God's instructions, Joshua leads the Israelites into the Promised Land.

◆ **Set the Course**

Our growing faith in God helps us step out in courage and obey him.

◆ **Bible Verse**

"Now faith is being sure of what we hope for and certain of what we do not see."
Hebrews 11:1

Workshop Objectives

What You'll Do, What You'll Need

1. Lead the kids on "Israel's Musical Journey," a musical retelling of the battle of Jericho.

__ 1 or 2 sets of "Boom Whackers" tuned percussion tubes
__ children's hand bells or other instruments
__ kazoos (7 per week)
__ 1 xylophone and mallet
__ signs with the following words on them:
BOOM WHACKERS, BELLS; KAZOO KHORUS; XYLOPHONE; YAHWEH!!!
Tip: Laminate the signs for future use.

2. Use the reflection questions to help kids grasp the concept of faith.

3. Play a fast-paced game of "Scriptionary" to reinforce the elements of the story where Joshua and the Israelites displayed faith.

__ 2 or 3 flip charts on stands (depending on class size)
__ markers
__ 2 or 3 scooters
__ 2 or 3 handbells
__ index cards with the following prompts on them:
• Manna Falling from Heaven
• Angel of the Lord
• River Jordan with Dry Path
• Memorial of Stones
• Marching Around the Walls of Jericho
• Blowing the Ram's Horn Trumpets
• Israelite's Shouting
• Walls Falling Down

Faith in Motion
◆Workshop Objectives

L E A R N I N G   T A S K S

Kids will:

 participate in the storytelling by providing sound effects with Boom Whackers, Bells, Kazoos and a Xylophone.
(knowledge, comprehension, application, analysis; Musical/Rhythmic, Bodily/Kinesthetic, Verbal/Linguistic, Interpersonal)

 reflect on the story and what it teaches them about faith.
(knowledge, comprehension, application, analysis; Verbal/Linguistic, Intrapersonal)

 play a fast-paced game of "Scriptionary" to reinforce the elements of the story that display the faith of the Israelites.
(knowledge, comprehension, application, analysis, synthesis; Bodily/Kinesthetic, Visual/Spatial, Interpersonal)

S P I R I T U A L   F O R M A T I O N

Kids will:

 learn the scriptural "definition" of faith by memorizing Hebrews 11:1.
(knowledge, comprehension)

 understand that our faith grows as we explore who Scripture reveals God to be and as we experience his faithfulness in our lives.
(knowledge, comprehension, application)

 understand that faith is fortified as we remember God's faithfulness in our lives and the lives of others.
(knowledge, comprehension, application, analysis)

 understand that the Israelites demonstrated their faith in obeying God's strange instructions for the defeat of Jericho and apply this lesson to their own lives as they learn to listen to God and obey his instruction.
(knowledge, comprehension, application, analysis, synthesis)

 understand that it is important to place our trust in God, not in the power (walls) of the world.
(knowledge, comprehension, application, analysis, synthesis)

Y e a r   o f   F a i t h

 Joshua: Courageous Faith

In the Zone

◆Israel's Musical Journey

ξ Post the BOOM WHACKERS, BELLS, KAZOO KHORUS, XYLOPHONE and
YAHWEH!!! signs on the wall or on a rolling bulletin board so everyone can see them.
You will point to the signs during your storytelling to prompt the groups to play.

ξ Before you begin your storytelling, set up a table and have the kids playing
boom whackers gently hit their tubes on the sides of the table. Let kids come up with a
pattern or rhythm and practice it with the boom whackers.

ξ Assign instruments and give instructions to each instrument group.

BOOM WHACKERS: (These are tuned percussion tubes that play a note when they strike a hard surface. Remind the kids that despite their fun appearance, they are musical instruments, not weapons.) **During the story, you'll play your rhythm whenever I point to the BOOM WHACKERS sign. For example: "The Israelites *marched, marched, marched* wherever God led them."**

HAND BELLS: **Hold the bells by the handle and ring them gently, unless I tell you to play harder. You'll ring the bells to accompany the story when I point to the BELLS sign. Let's practice. "While they slept, small white flakes called manna *rained, rained, rained* on the ground."**

KAZOOS: In order to keep from sharing germs, you'll need to use one kazoo per child. Use half the kazoos in Act One, and half in Act Two so the kazoo players can switch instruments. **In Act One, the Kazoo Khorus plays a trumpet sound, *da-da-da-daaa!* every time I say "priest." In Act Two, the Kazoo Khorus plays every time**

the trumpet blows. I'll point to the KAZOO sign, so heads up! For example: "God told Joshua to tell the PRIESTS *(da-da-da-daaa!)* to carry the Ark of the Covenant into the River Jordan."

XYLOPHONE: Assign two xylophone players, one for Act One and one for Act Two. Or, have a shepherd play the xylophone for both acts. **Watch me and run the mallet all the way up the keys when I point to the XYLOPHONE sign.**

Now we're all set! Watch for your cues and get ready to add some zip and zing to our story. If I run my finger across my throat like this (demonstrate), **that means to stop playing and listen. Remember, you'll get to switch instruments for Act Two.**

Tell the story dramatically to keep the children interested in the content rather than just anticipating when they are going to play. The script is coded to help you prompt the groups to play as you tell the story.

Joshua Faith in Motion

3

⬩Act One

Our story begins in the desert where the nation of Israel, all two million men, women and children, wandered for 40 years after God rescued them from Egypt. The Israelites **(BW) marched, marched, marched** wherever God led them. After each long journey, they would stop, set up camp and sleep. **(X)** While they slept, small white flakes called manna **(B) rained and rained and rained** onto the ground. The people gathered enough manna to eat each day. It tasted delicious—like wafers made with honey!

Moses lived to be an old man. After leading the Israelites for 40 years, Moses died. Joshua became the new leader of God's people. He told them it was time to cross into the land God had promised them. The people packed up their tents and **(BW) marched, marched, marched** toward Canaan. They arrived at the banks of the River Jordan. In summer, this river could **(B) babble, babble, babble** along. But when the Israelites got there, it was spring and the river was overflowing its banks. It **(BW) rushed, rushed, rushed** through the valley. "How will we cross?" the people wondered. There was no bridge, there were no boats.

> **(BW)**
> **Boom Whackers**
>
> **(B) Bells**
>
> **(KK)**
> **Kazoo Khorus**
>
> **(X)**
> **Xylophone**

The water was SOOOO high! God told Joshua to tell the **(KK) priests** to carry the Ark of the Covenant into the River Jordan. Joshua looked at the river as it **(BW) rushed, rushed, rushed** through the valley. The **(KK) priests** looked at the river as it **(BW) rushed, rushed, rushed** through the valley. They may have had their doubts; they may have been afraid of what would happen, but they decided to trust God's directions. The **(KK) priests** stepped in the water and it just dried up.**(X)** The people **(B) tiptoed, tiptoed, tiptoed** into the river bed. When they realized it was safe, they **(BW) marched, marched, marched** across while the **(KK) priests** stood in the middle of the dry river, holding the Ark of the Covenant.

Joshua commanded 12 men, one from each tribe of Israel, to pick up huge stones from the center of the dry riverbed. The men picked up the stones, **(B) smooth, smooth, smooth** stones and **(BW) stacked, stacked, stacked** them all together to build a reminder that they could trust in God, even when the situation looked impossible. When the memorial was built, the **(KK) priests** stepped out of the river and the water **(BW) rushed, rushed, rushed** back into place. The Israelites were in the Promised Land! **(X)**

⬩Act Two

The Israelites camped at Gilgal, near the tall strong walls of Jericho. One day, while Joshua was walking, the angel of the Lord appeared to him. **(X)** The angel **(X)** gave Joshua the battle plan for defeating Jericho. He would march around the city, **(KK) blowing trumpets!** This probably seemed like a very weird plan to Joshua. How could he be certain it would work? The truth is, there were no guarantees. Joshua just had to have faith, to trust that God would bring down the walls as he promised.

Joshua assembled the men who would march against Jericho. Heading the procession were 20,000 armed men. They **(BW)** marched, marched, marched toward Jericho. Next came the priests, **(KK) blowing** ram's horn trumpets and carrying the Ark of the Covenant. Following the priests came the rear guard, 20,000 more armed men who **(B) stomped, stomped, stomped** toward Jericho. They arrived at the city walls, **(X)** which were closed up tight in fear and dread. At Joshua's command, the Israelites circled the city. The front guard **(BW) marched, marched, marched** while the **priests (KK) blew the trumpets**, and the rear guard **(B) stomped, stomped, stomped** behind the **priests.**

(BW) Boom Whackers

(B) Bells

(KK) Kazoo Khorus

(X) Xylophone

They circled the city once, then they returned to camp for the night. **(X)** This was their routine for six days. Did the Israelites see any sense to this battle plan? Probably not. Were there moments when they doubted, when their faith grew weak? Probably. But still they chose to trust God and they marched.

The seventh day was different from the first six. On the seventh day they circled the city seven times. The seventh time around, the front guard **(BW) marched, marched, marched,** the priests **(KK) blew the trumpets,** and the rear guard **(B) stomped, stomped, stomped** behind the priests. Until this point, they had been silent. No one spoke a word.

But on this day, the seventh day, Joshua had given them special instructions. When he gave the word, they were all to shout. What did they shout that day? No one knows for sure. But since God's strength, not man's, was in control, perhaps they shouted the holy name of God—**YAHWEH.** Say it with me: **YAHWEH.** So…when Joshua gave the order, the priests **(KK) blew and blew and blew** and everyone shouted **YAHWEH** and the walls came **(BW, B, KK, X) tumbling and rumbling and crashing down!** The Israelites climbed over the rubble and into the city. God gave them the victory just like that!

2 ◆ Reflection

Have kids put the instruments away and join you in a group.

Our unit memory verse is Hebrew 11:1. It tells us that "Faith is being sure of what we hope for and certain of what we do not see." Say that with me. Lead kids phrase by phrase. **Let's look at our story today and explore this definition of faith a little further.**

☆ **What do you think the Israelites hoped for when they saw the rushing water of the Jordan River?**

☆ **Do you think they were absolutely sure that God would make a path like He did when their ancestors crossed the Red Sea?**

☆ **How do you think they felt about God's plan to defeat Jericho?**

✩ **Do you think having faith means you never have doubts?** (We want the kids to realize that faith means trusting God even when you do have doubts. What we can be certain about is that God loves us and wants what is best for us.)

✩ **What does God want you to do when you doubt?** (Trust him.)

3 ◆ Scriptionary

≈ Set up flip charts with markers at one end of the room.

≈ Form two or three teams, depending on the size of your class. With eight prompt cards, 24 kids can play on three teams. Add other prompts if your class is bigger than 24. Yikes!

≈ Assemble the teams facing the flip charts at the other end of the room. Place a bell in front of each team.

Explain the rules.

One member of each team will sit on a scooter facing the rest of his/her team. I will show the first student in each group the same index card prompt. At my signal, those people will look at the prompt without letting anyone on the team see it. They must then turn around to face the flip chart and scooter to the flip chart. When they arrive at the flip chart, they quickly draw a picture to help their teams guess what part of the story they are illustrating. No words or numbers may be used.

Only the next team member in each line may guess what is being drawn. When he/she discovers the clue, he/she should pick up and ring the bell and announce the identity of the clue. We'll play until all prompts have been drawn. Everyone's a winner, even if one team guesses correctly more often than others.

Collect the markers and bells and gather kids in a group. Congratulate them on their efforts. All of the things you drew displayed times that the Israelites had to have faith. They had no guarantees, but they trusted God's plan.

Close with prayer. Dear Lord, Help us to trust you even when we don't understand. Help us to have faith even when your plan may be very different from our own. In Jesus' name, Amen.

Sunday School isn't about

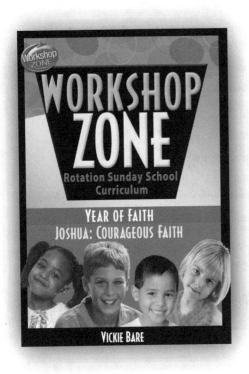

Sunday School has always been about finding the best possible ways to reach children with the life-changing message expressed in God's Word.

Multidimensional/rotation learning is not something entirely new. Rather, it is a fresh paradigm based on our growing understanding of how kids learn. Its purpose is simply to make disciples, as Jesus instructed, by giving kids memorable experiences with the Word.

What drives us to find new, creative ways to present the Bible to kids? Simply this. Each year we learn more and more about how God has programmed us to learn. As we utilize the multiple pathways God has put at our disposal, the impact of our teaching takes on a whole new dynamic. The question before each of us is: "Are we using all the intelligences to convey the message of God's story, to let it sink deep into children's minds and hearts?" Spending weeks on the same story gives children the maximum opportunity to experience the story in ways that will expand their knowledge of God and grow their tender, young faith. So while the workshop rotation model may provide the richest learning environment, there are many ways to be "multidimensional" in teaching God's Word.

lectures anymore.

Made up of nine four-week long units, the first year of curriculum, the Year of Faith leads kids in an exploration of different kinds of faith exhibited by key Bible characters.

- 0781442133 - Joshua: Courageous Faith
- 0781442141 - David: Faith vs. Force
- 078144215X - Faith in the Furnace
- 0781442168 - Faith Finds the Messiah
- 0781442176 - Daniel: Faith Faces Lions
- 0781442184 - A Lame Man Healed: Faith Goes Through the Roof
- 0781442192 - Peter: Faith with Wet Feet
- 0781442206 - Resurrection Faith
- 0781442214 - Paul and Silas: Faith in Prison

The 8 workshops in each unit of the Year of Faith are:

Good Shepherd's Inn
Kids settle into a cozy atmosphere and enjoy a Bible storyteller drama, then make and munch a yummy snack that ties in to the story.

Salt and Light Shop
Science and nature exploration leads to wonderful discoveries about our Creator and the stories he gives us to live by.

Mountaintop Productions
The tantalizing smell of popcorn welcomes kids to this workshop where they view and analyze clips that expand the scope of the Bible story.

Faith in Motion
Here's a chance to get rowdy with lively games that challenge kids to recall and relate to important points of the story.

Seaside Studio
For the artist in every child! Kids create personal artistic expressions of their spiritual growth and response to the Bible story.

Stargazer Theater
Let kids be the stars! This workshop sets the stage for Bible study through all kinds of performing arts—puppets, music and drama.

Temple Court
With a focus on spiritual formation, kids openly explore and express their growing faith with real life responses.

Game Zone
Put those growing minds to the test with an interactive Bible story review followed by fun and fascinating game shows such as Holy Word Squares, Bible Jeopardy, Who Wants to Be a Bible Scholar and more!

So, go ahead ... be daring ... take your kids on a multidimensional field trip through the Bible ... and watch them learn!!!

The Word at Work . . . Around the World

 hat would you do if you wanted to share God's love with children on the streets of your city? That's the dilemma David C. Cook faced in 1870s Chicago. His answer was to create literature that would capture children's hearts.

Out of those humble beginnings grew a worldwide ministry that has used literature to proclaim God's love and disciple generation after generation. Cook Communications Ministries is committed to personal discipleship—to helping people of all ages learn God's Word, embrace his salvation, walk in his ways, and minister in his name.

Opportunities—and Crisis

We live in a land of plenty—including plenty of Christian literature! But what about the rest of the world? Jesus commanded, "Go and make disciples of all nations" (Matt. 28:19) and we want to obey this commandment. But how does a publishing organization "go" into all the world?

There are five times as many Christians around the world as there are in North America. Christian workers in many of these countries have no more than a New Testament, or perhaps a single shared copy of the Bible, from which to learn and teach.

We are committed to sharing what God has given us with such Christians.

A vital part of Cook Communications Ministries is our international outreach, Cook Communications Ministries International (CCMI). Your purchase of this book, and of other books and Christian-growth products from Cook, enables CCMI to provide Bibles and Christian literature to people in more than 150 languages in 65 countries.

Cook Communications Ministries is a not-for-profit, self-supporting organization. Revenues from sales of our books, Bible curriculum, and other church and home products not only fund our U.S. ministry, but also fund our CCMI ministry around the world. One hundred percent of donations to CCMI go to our international literature programs.

CCMI reaches out internationally in three ways:

· Our premier International Christian Publishing Institute (ICPI) trains leaders from nationally led publishing houses around the world to develop evangelism and discipleship materials to transform lives in their countries.

· We provide literature for pastors, evangelists, and Christian workers in their national language. We provide study helps for pastors and lay leaders in many parts of the world, such as China, India, Cuba, Iran, and Vietnam.

· We reach people at risk—refugees, AIDS victims, street children, and famine victims—with God's Word. CCMI puts literature that shares the Good News into the hands of people at spiritual risk—people who might die before they hear the name of Jesus and are transformed by his love.

Word Power—God's Power

Faith Kidz, RiverOak, Honor, Life Journey, Victor, NexGen — every time you purchase a book produced by Cook Communications Ministries, you not only meet a vital personal need in your life or in the life of someone you love, but you're also a part of ministering to José in Colombia, Humberto in Chile, Gousa in India, or Lidiane in Brazil. You help make it possible for a pastor in China, a child in Peru, or a mother in West Africa to enjoy a life-changing book. And because you helped, children and adults around the world are learning God's Word and walking in his ways.

Thank you for your partnership in helping to disciple the world. May God bless you with the power of his Word in your life.

For more information about our international ministries, visit www.ccmi.org.